Oxford School Shakespeare

# Julius Caesar

edited by

**Roma Gill**
M.A. *Cantab*. B.Litt. *Oxon*.
Reader in English Literature
University of Sheffield

Oxford University Press

Oxford University Press, Walton Street, Oxford OX2 6DP
London Glasgow New York Toronto
Delhi Bombay Calcutta Madras Karachi
Kuala Lumpur Singapore Hong Kong Tokyo
Nairobi Dar es Salaam Cape Town
Melbourne Auckland
and associated companies in
Beirut Berlin Ibadan Mexico City Nicosia

Oxford is a trade mark of Oxford University Press

First published 1979
Reprinted 1980, 1982 (twice), 1983

Illustrations by Coral Mula

For Richard

**Oxford School Shakespeare**
*edited by Roma Gill*

A Midsummer Night's Dream
Romeo and Juliet
As You Like It
Macbeth
Julius Caesar
The Merchant of Venice

Printed in Great Britain
at the University Press, Oxford
by Eric Buckley
Printer to the University

# A letter to all students of this text

I want to say a few words of explanation to all those readers who are studying this text for examination purposes. I'm sure that Shakespeare would be very pleased with the kind of attention that you and I are going to give to the words of his play—but he would also be very surprised. He wrote his plays to be *acted*. He did not think that they would be *read*—and read more than 300 years after he had written them. He cared so little for *readers*, that many of his plays were not printed until after his death.

Act this play! Enjoy the characters, the situations, and the language. Don't worry too much if you don't fully understand the language at first. A modern poet, T. S. Eliot, has said that the best poetry will mean *something* to the reader before it is completely understood.

Shakespeare wrote the best poetry; but his language is not easy to appreciate, even for those who are native speakers of English. There are three reasons for this.

Firstly, you will find that some words look odd because there is an apostrophe where you would expect a letter: the word 'ever', for instance, often appears as 'e'er'. Many verbs appear in the past tense as (for example) 'look'd' which you have been properly taught to spell 'looked'. This is because of the length of Shakespeare's verse line, which has ten syllables (when it is regular). By writing 'e'er' and not 'ever' the dramatist managed to save one syllable. It is almost the same with verbs in the past tense. Although today 'looked' is pronounced as one syllable, in Shakespeare's time it could have been two—'look-ed'. The spelling 'look'd' instructs you to use a modern English pronunciation. When you find 'looked' in poetry, you should pronounce the second syllable as well as the first. This care for the rhythm of the lines is not needed in the prose parts of the play, and so the spelling there is the spelling of modern English.

The second problem is that we no longer speak the English of Shakespeare's time. Many words have changed their meaning. When Jaques in *As You Like It* calls Touchstone 'A material fool' (*Act 3*, Scene 3, line 28), we need to be told that 'material' here means 'full of ideas', and that Jaques is saying that although Touchstone is a fool, he is by no means stupid.

Finally, it is sometimes hard to understand what a character is saying. This is because Shakespeare had a very powerful mind, and his thoughts are not always easy to understand. As well as this, he liked to play with words, as we see when Macbeth murmurs to himself

If it were done when 'tis done, then 'twere well
It were done quickly.                                        (*1*, 8, 1–2)

Macbeth is thinking of murdering his king, and he plays with the different meanings of the word 'done'. He is saying that if the business of the murder was *ended* ('done') as soon as it was *performed* ('done'), then it would be a good thing that it should be *carried out* ('done') as soon as possible. In the rest of the play Shakespeare shows us that the murder was not completed when the king died, but that Macbeth was forced to kill more people in order to hide his first crime. At the same time, he had to recognize his guilt, and bear his punishment.

Don't think a lot about the past. It is true that Shakespeare was writing in the sixteenth and early seventeenth centuries, as you will see from the Table on p. 113. Yet soon after his death Ben Jonson, who was a friend of Shakespeare's and a playwright himself, said of him that 'He was not of an age, but for all time'. The characters that Shakespeare has created, and the feelings that he has described, are alive in *our* world. You must know of girls who are in love, of men who are politically ambitious, and of misers who only care about money. These, and many more, are the characters in Shakespeare's plays.

Study this play then; and act it. Read it aloud. You owe it to yourselves and to your teachers to do as well as you can in the examinations. You also have a debt to Shakespeare, and you can pay this debt by *acting* the play, and enjoying it—just as he intended it to be acted, and enjoyed. You need no fancy costumes or expensive scenery. Shakespeare's own professional actors had very little scenery. Their clothes had often been given to them by rich courtiers who were tired of them. There were no women among these actors, for it was not thought respectable for a woman to act. Boys played the parts of the female characters.

This play is given to you as it would be given to a company of actors. You are told when each character comes on to the stage ('*Enter* Macbeth'), and when he leaves ('*Exit*'). It is traditional in the theatre to use Latin here, saying 'exit' for 'he goes out' or 'exeunt' for 'they go out'. Sometimes you will find a stage direction telling you that a noise is heard 'within'. This simply means that the noise is off-stage. Very often a scene is introduced with music, or with the sound of trumpets if a king is to enter. This music is like the soundtrack of a film: it helps the audience to find the proper mood for the action.

In the Introduction and the Notes I have tried to help you as much as I can. But I may well have missed something that you could tell me about. If this happens, please write to me at the local office of the Oxford University Press. Your letters will be forwarded to me, and I shall be very happy to hear from you.

Roma Gill

# Contents

# Shakespeare and the Romans

Shakespeare read of the murder of Julius Caesar in a history book, Plutarch's *Lives of the Greeks and Romans*. This was written in Latin during the first century after the birth of Christ. Plutarch's Latin was translated into French by James Amyot, and then in 1579 Sir Thomas North translated the French into English. I have printed a selection of passages[1] from North's translation at the end of the play, so that you can read some of the story that inspired Shakespeare, and also compare the prose narrative with the play. For instance, Plutarch mentioned the detail of Caesar's dislike of thin men (p. 95), and this becomes verse in *Act 1*, scene 2, lines 191–4. You can see how a dramatist works when Shakespeare takes the account of the killing of Cinna (p. 98) and invents words to be spoken by the nameless 'common people', in *Act 3*, scene 3. Most remarkable of all is the way Shakespeare interprets Plutarch's few hints about the tone and content of Antony's funeral oration for Caesar (p. 97) to construct the famous speech, 'Friends, Romans, countrymen', that the play's Antony makes to the citizens (3, 2, 75–253).

Occasionally in discussing the characters of Caesar and Brutus I have made reference to Plutarch's history. The details that Shakespeare borrows from his source are always of interest, but it is even more fascinating to notice the differences between the history and the play. What Shakespeare changes, or ignores, or invents can be very helpful when we try to understand the characters as the author intended them to be understood.

Writing for a stage performance allowed Shakespeare to ignore the actual times at which these historical events occurred. Caesar made his triumphal entry into Rome in 45 B.C.; he was assassinated in March the following year. Octavius was hostile to Antony for more than a year after the assassination, but finally joined forces with him and Lepidus in 43 B.C. The conspirators were defeated at Philippi in 42 B.C. Shakespeare's play starts with a scene in which the crowd waits eagerly for Caesar's entry into Rome; from here until the day of the murder in *Act 3*, scene 1, there is no break in the action. The Elizabethan theatre had no curtains, and no division

---

[1] I have taken the passages from *Shakespeare's Plutarch*, ed. T. J. B. Spencer (London, 1964); page numbers from this edition are given with the passages.

was marked (as it is in a printed text) between one scene and the next. Once or twice we are made aware that *some* time is passing, but we have no sense of hours, days, or months. As a result, causes seem to be very closely linked with their effects. Immediately we have heard Cassius plotting to hide letters where Brutus will find them (*1*, 3, 142–6), we are shown Brutus, in his study, being given and reading one of the mysterious letters.

We often make a fuss today about the historical accuracy of theatrical scenery and costumes. Shakespeare had no such worries. A little scenery was perhaps available to the actors, but we have no means of knowing how they indicated, for example, the Capitol. But in *Act 3*, scene 1 we hear Cassius reproaching Artemidorus—

> What! urge you your petitions in the street?
> Come to the Capitol;                                        (lines 11–12)

this is enough to tell us that we are, for the moment, 'in the street'. Later in the scene, Caesar announces that he is ready to listen to petitions (line 31), and so we know that the scene has changed, slightly, and that we have been taken to the Capitol. In the matter of costume, it is clear that Shakespeare did not think of the Romans as we think of them. He shows us Cassius 'unbraced'—that is, with his doublet unfastened (*1*, 3, 48); and he makes Brutus discover a book with 'the leaf turn'd down / Where I left reading' (*4*, 3, 272–3). An Elizabethan would wear a doublet and read a book: the Roman wore a toga and read from a scroll (see illustration on p. 16). A clock strikes on two occasions in the play (*2*, 1, 191 and *2*, 2, 114); but striking clocks had not been invented in the time of Julius Caesar. These anachronisms—the placing of objects in the wrong period—are sometimes said to show Shakespeare's ignorance or carelessness, but this makes them too important. The striking clock adds urgency to the scene; Brutus with his book and Cassius in his doublet would seem familiar figures to the Elizabethans—men of their own time and type, instead of foreigners from a remote past.

> How many ages hence
> Shall this our lofty scene be acted o'er,
> In states unborn and accents yet unknown.      (*3*, 1, 111–13)

This prophetic utterance is made by Shakespeare's character, not by the historical Cassius; he speaks the truth. The play gives new life to a series of historical events and persons, and, by doing this, rescues them from antiquity. The pride of Caesar, the love of Antony, and the conflict in Brutus between personal and public loyalties are as real today as they were two thousand years ago. Nevertheless, an outline of the historical and political background to the events in Rome between 45 B.C. and 42 B.C. will help you to understand Shakespeare's play better; it is especially necessary for the understanding of Brutus's dilemma.

In the sixth century before the birth of Christ, Rome was ruled by a king, Tarquin the Proud. He was a brutal tyrant, and the people, under the leadership of Lucius Junius Brutus, rebelled against him, deposed him, and in 509 B.C. established Rome as a republic. From that time, Rome was governed by two consuls, who were elected by the people; their authority was equal, and they remained in power for one year only. They acted upon advice from the Senate, which had originally been the king's council and which was composed entirely of men who had held some state office. Tribunes, elected from the body of the citizens, kept watch over the Senate, to protect the rights of the common people.

Eventually, however, this political structure began to weaken, and early in the first century B.C. three men—Pompey, Crassus, and Julius Caesar—united to form a triumvirate (from the Latin *tres viri*) to govern Rome and its provinces. In 53 B.C. Crassus was killed whilst fighting the Parthians (in the battle where Cassius captured Pindarus; see 5, 3, 37). Neither Pompey nor Caesar would agree to share power with the other, and so civil war broke out. At the battle of Pharsalia (48 B.C.) Caesar defeated Pompey; then, a little later, he conquered Pompey's two sons. The play opens with Caesar's return from this last victory.

Caesar now appeared to have absolute power, but the name of 'king' was hated and feared in Rome. Yet Caesar was popular. He was brave, successful, and generous; and the citizens loved him. But some of the senators and aristocracy were afraid that he would become a tyrant (like Tarquin) and make slaves of the people. Chief among these senators were Marcus Brutus (a descendant of Lucius Junius Brutus) and Cassius. In the civil war they had both fought on Pompey's side against Caesar, but Caesar had pardoned and befriended Brutus and, at Brutus's request, recalled Cassius to Rome.

After the murder of Julius Caesar, full democracy never again returned to Rome. A second triumvirate was formed, this time consisting of Antony, Lepidus, and Octavius Caesar. Lepidus was the weak link (as Antony tells us in 4, 1, 12-40); and Antony himself was well known to be 'a masker and a reveller' (as Cassius taunts him in 5, 1, 62). Only Octavius, called a 'peevish schoolboy' by Cassius (5, 1, 61) because he was only eighteen at the time of the murder, was able to sustain his role as one of the three rulers of the great Roman empire. Octavius was Julius Caesar's great-nephew and heir; he adopted the name 'Caesar', with the addition of 'Augustus', and these titles were ever afterwards bestowed upon Roman rulers. In 27 B.C. Octavius took the further title of 'Princeps'—the chief one; and Rome ceased to be a republic.

# Leading characters in the play

**Julius Caesar**  The greatest and most powerful of the Romans, and the last of the three men who formed the first triumvirate (see p. ix). He is assassinated by a band of conspirators led by Brutus and Cassius, who believe that Caesar is ambitious to be made king. See also p. xiii.

**Calphurnia**  The wife of Julius Caesar; she is worried about her husband's well-being, and her prophetic dream foretells the assassination.

**Octavius Caesar**  The great-nephew of Julius Caesar, heir to his uncle's wealth and position. He joins Mark Antony in making war on the conspirators.

**Mark Antony**  Caesar's loyal friend. His funeral oration for Caesar is calculated not only to praise the dead man, but also to incite the citizens to mutiny against the murderers. Antony joins Octavius Caesar and Lepidus to form the second triumvirate (see p. ix), and together they lead an attack on the conspirators and defeat them at Philippi.

**Marcus Brutus**  Caesar's great friend, who joins in the conspiracy because his love for Rome is even greater than his love for his friend. He is an idealist, and believes that other men have the same high principles as himself; this leads him to make errors of judgement which ultimately result in the defeat at Philippi. See also p. xxv.

**Portia**  The wife of Brutus; she is devoted to her husband and distressed by his anxiety. Through her we see another aspect of Brutus—the gentle, loving husband. Portia is the daughter of Marcus Cato, who preferred to kill himself rather than be captured by Julius Caesar when Pompey was defeated; Portia shows the influence of her father's Stoic philosophy in her apparent indifference to physical suffering.

**Cassius**  The inspirer and organizer of the conspiracy against Caesar, whom he hates. He is a fanatic, but he is also a practical man, well aware of his own limitations and those of other men. At first Cassius is not a very attractive character, but he becomes more noble—even heroic—in his defeat.

Casca    He is prominent among the conspirators, not because he is a
         strongly-drawn character but because Shakespeare uses him in so
         many different ways: he scoffs at the ceremony with the crown;
         he is superstitious in the storm; and he strikes the first blow in the
         murder of Caesar.

# Julius Caesar—'the foremost man of all this world'

In Shakespeare's play we hear a lot *about* Julius Caesar—he is praised by Mark Antony; Brutus loves him; Cassius hates him; and the Roman citizens change in their feelings towards him from admiration to dislike, then back again to respect and love. We see, however, very little of the man himself: he appears in only three scenes. In *Act 1*, scene 2 he enters twice, each time walking in procession from one side of the stage to the other, and making brief comments as he passes. The first entrance shows him as a man of authority, accustomed to unquestioning obedience: 'When Caesar says "Do this", it is perform'd' (*1*, 2, 10). On the second occasion he speaks of his suspicions of Cassius; we know that these are well-founded, and we approve his judgement. In *Act 2*, scene 2 Caesar is at home, listening to his wife's worries about his safety. He also is anxious; at first he refuses to show fear, then he is persuaded not to go to the Capitol, and finally he yields to Decius' argument—perhaps because, as his enemies have claimed, he is ambitious to be crowned king.

Caesar's last appearance is in the Capitol on the ides of March —the day that a Soothsayer has warned him to avoid. He firmly refuses to repeal a sentence of banishment, and this refusal is the cue for the conspirators. They stab, and Caesar dies.

We have seen, then, a man of authority, brave, and possibly ambitious—but we cannot feel that we *know* Caesar, or understand him, from these quick glimpses of his character. We have seen the 'public' man, rather than the 'private' one. And yet, Mark Antony's praise does not seem extravagant when he says that Caesar was 'the noblest man / That ever lived in the tide of time' (*3*, 1, 256–7). We are certain of this, not because the play has presented us with a great man, but because even before we began to read *Julius Caesar*, we knew Caesar's name—even though we were perhaps unable to say exactly *why* he was so famous. The Elizabethan education system, however, made sure that Shakespeare's contemporaries were very well informed about such matters. Latin was the main subject in every school, and pupils studied the history as well as the language and literature of Rome. There was no need for Shakespeare to record Caesar's achievements, and he most certainly did not need to invent fictions when the facts were both familiar and dramatic. Today, many more subjects are taught in schools, and we cannot afford so much time to study the great contribution made by the Romans to English culture. For this reason—and not because Shakespeare failed in his creation of the character—explanations are necessary. We have to do our homework before we read *Julius Caesar*.

Julius Caesar was born in 100 B.C., and before he was twenty years old he had become a distinguished soldier. In the course of a glittering military and political career, he fought and held office in Africa, Spain and France, and he extended Roman rule to the Atlantic and to the English Channel. He was renowned both as general and as statesman. With Crassus and Pompey he formed the first triumvirate in 60 B.C.; then the death of Crassus in 53 B.C. and the defeat of Pompey in 48 B.C. gave him the power of an autocrat. In the intervals between military campaigns he devoted himself with amazing energy, to re-establishing order in Rome, improving the economic situation, regulating taxation, codifying the law, and instituting a public library.

Caesar was also a gifted writer. His *Commentaries* on the Gallic Wars and on the Civil War are masterpieces of narrative skill. Other writings have not survived, but we know that they included a textbook of grammar (written during a journey across the Alps), and a work on the stars. He was an expert astronomer and mathematician, and the calendar that he devised in 46 B.C. is the one we use today; in his honour, one of the months was renamed Julius—July.

Every single one of these achievements is, in its own way, a triumph; when they are considered together, and recognized as the contribution made to civilization *by one man*, it is hard to find appropriate words of praise. We can only agree with Brutus that the man he has murdered was indeed 'the foremost man of all this world' (4, 3, 22).

With the assistance of Plutarch's *Life of Caesar* we can be sure how Shakespeare intended us to regard the character. Plutarch is not, on the whole, sympathetic to Caesar: he speaks of Caesar's pride, which made him act as though he were a god, and of 'the covetous desire he had to be called king', which gave the Roman citizens 'just cause . . . to bear him ill will' (page 81). In the play, however, Shakespeare has ignored most of this. Only Cassius refers to Caesar's god-like behaviour (1, 2, 115 ff.), and he is not to be trusted. Caesar is persuaded by Decius to go to the Capitol (2, 2, 93 ff.), but it is not clear whether he is tempted by the promise of a crown, or afraid of being laughed at if he stays at home. And the first scene of the play shows that the people, far from bearing him 'ill will', are eager 'to see Caesar, and to rejoice in his triumph' (*1*, 1, 34).

The long description of Caesar given by Cassius (*1*, 2, 100–31) is remarkable for what it tells us of the speaker, and not for its revelation of Caesar. On one occasion, we learn, Caesar almost drowned; at another time, he was very ill. Cassius speaks of physical weakness as though it were moral weakness, interpreting the shivering and pallor of fever as the trembling and bloodlessness of fear. In fact, Caesar's struggles against his disability made his achievements appear even more triumphant; even Plutarch admitted this, recounting how Caesar

> yielded not to the sickness of his body, to make it a cloak to cherish him withal, but, contrarily, took the pains of war as a medicine to cure his sick body, fighting always with his disease.                                      (page 37)

Cassius shows his own mean spirit, which is shared by Casca when he scoffs at the epileptic fit that embarrassed Caesar in the market-place (*1*, 2, 246ff.).

A small incident that Shakespeare alters from Plutarch is Caesar's reception of the letter from Artemidorus. In the historical source, Caesar accepts the letter,

> but could never read it, though he many times attempted it, for the number of people that did salute him.          (page 91)

The alteration in the play is significant. Artemidorus presses Caesar to take the letter and read it:

> O Caesar, read mine first; for mine's a suit
> That touches Caesar nearer. Read it, great Caesar.

With dignity, Caesar rejects the letter:

> What touches us ourself shall be last serv'd.          (*3*, 1, 6–8)

Unselfishness, and not the throng of people, puts Caesar's life at risk; this alteration to Plutarch's account should direct our total response to Shakespeare's Caesar.

Caesar is murdered at the beginning of Act 3, and you may at first think it odd that the hero should vanish from the stage before the play is half-finished. But although the man is dead, his spirit lives on. It is present in the minds of those who murdered him, and of those who seek to avenge the murder. We are so conscious of this unseen presence that it is no surprise when the spirit materializes, and the ghost of Caesar appears to Brutus before the battle at Philippi. Brutus does not seem surprised either: when the ghost tells him 'thou shalt see me at Philippi', his reply is one of calm acceptance: 'Why, I will see thee at Philippi then' (4, 3, 282, 284).

The tragedy of *Julius Caesar* is not the tragedy of one man alone. Brutus shares the tragic fate—and so too does Cassius, although to a lesser extent. The tragedy was not completed when Caesar died in the Capitol, and Brutus makes this plain when he talks to Cassius before Philippi:

> this same day
> Must end that work the ides of March begun. (5, 1, 112–13)

# *Julius Caesar*: the play

## Act 1

Scene 1  Flavius and Marullus are annoyed when they find that the Roman citizens have taken a holiday from work and are crowding on to the streets 'to see Caesar, and to rejoice in his triumph'. A cobbler tries to joke with the tribunes, but they are too angry to laugh. Marullus reproaches the people for their disloyalty: they have forgotten their love for Pompey, and now Caesar is their hero. The blank verse and dignified language of the tribune's speech contrasts with the cobbler's colloquial prose, and mark a kind of class distinction between the major characters in the play (who are identified by name), and the ordinary citizens, the men-in-the-street.

When they hear what Marullus has to say, the people are silent and slink away from the scene. Flavius explains what is happening:

> See whe'r their basest mettle be not mov'd;
> They vanish tongue-tied in their guiltiness.

The Roman citizens are very important in *Julius Caesar*, and provide an essential background to the action. They are influenced by emotion, not by reason, and their affections are not to be trusted: in the past they cheered for Pompey; now they are welcoming Caesar, the man who has defeated Pompey; and soon we shall hear them applauding the men who have murdered Caesar.

Flavius and Marullus are determined to insult Caesar by tearing down the decorations intended to honour him. Their conversation gives us a hint of what is to come—we shall hear from other characters who also fear that Caesar will 'soar above the view of men / And keep us all in servile fearfulness'.

Scene 2  As the tribunes depart, Caesar's ceremonial procession enters, and we have a brief glimpse of the great man. The ominous words 'Beware the ides of March' are spoken, and then the procession leaves the stage. Brutus and Cassius stay behind. Very gently, Cassius tries to win Brutus's confidence. He flatters Brutus a little, then declares his own honesty. A shout from the crowds attending Caesar, offstage, startles Brutus, and he accidentally speaks his thoughts aloud: 'I do fear the people / Choose Caesar for their king'. The word 'fear' encourages Cassius to proceed with an attack on Caesar. He recalls two instances when Caesar showed weakness, but Cassius speaks as though the weakness were moral, and not merely physical. Cassius shows a mean spirit here, but Brutus does not seem to notice—or perhaps his attention is distracted by another shout from the crowd. Cassius returns to flattery, reminding Brutus of his own reputation and that of his ancestor, the Brutus who expelled Tarquin from Rome (see p. ix). At last Brutus promises that he will give some thought to the matters that Cassius has raised.

Some relaxation of tension is needed now, and it is supplied by Casca's account of the ceremony with the crown—'yet 'twas not a crown neither, 'twas one of these coronets'. Again there is a contrast between prose and verse, and between the colloquial, idiomatic language of Casca's speeches and the formal, dignified utterances of Brutus and Cassius.

When Cassius is alone, he points out how easily Brutus's nobility of character can be perverted; we realize, too, what a dangerous man Cassius is, and the threat to Caesar becomes very frightening:

> let Caesar seat him sure;
> For we will shake him, or worse days endure.

The threat is echoed in the thunder that heralds the next scene.

**Scene 3**   The storm renews the tension. Both the Romans and the Elizabethans believed that the world of Nature (the macrocosm) and the political world of human affairs (the microcosm) reflected each other, and that disturbances in one foretold, or paralleled, unusual events in the other. Of course, there were sceptics in both nations who denied that there was any link between the two worlds: Cicero is such a sceptic, but Casca is convinced that the storm is intended as a warning from the gods. Cassius, however, welcomes the storm, and shows his fanaticism as he walks unprotected. He interprets the night's unnatural events as being parallels to the monstrosity in the Roman world, and Casca understands: ''Tis Caesar that you mean; is it not, Cassius?'

Cassius tests Casca's feelings about Caesar, then invites him to take part in the conspiracy. When Cinna joins them, we learn that the plot is well advanced.

## Act 2

Scene 1

We now recognize that the play is operating on two time-scales. Cicero's opening remark in *Act 1*, scene 3 ('Good even, Casca: brought you Caesar home?') suggests that Casca has just left Caesar, having escorted him home after the celebrations of the Lupercal (*Act 1*, scene 2). When this scene ends, Cassius observes that 'it is after midnight'. The conspirators go in search of Brutus and find him at home, just as dawn is breaking ('yon grey lines / That fret the clouds are messengers of day'). But more than *hours* have elapsed. The storm gives an impression of continuity between *Act 1*, scene 3 and *Act 2*, scene 1; but we have in fact moved from 15 February (the feast of Lupercal) to 15 (the ides) March. Brutus has had weeks, not hours, in which to decide upon a course of action, and his soliloquy now reflects the thoughts of that whole period.

A soliloquy—words, not intended for a listener, spoken by a character when he is thinking aloud—is, by the conventions of Elizabethan drama, always to be trusted. Brutus now states his dilemma clearly: he has no personal grudge against Caesar, and no reason to distrust him—but, on the other hand, all power corrupts, and if Caesar is given imperial power, he may prove a danger to Rome. His honour and his patriotism urge Brutus to take action against Caesar, and although he recognizes the ugliness of the situation, he steps forward to welcome the conspirators. He shakes each one by the hand, speaking his name in token of fellowship (and incidentally introducing the different characters to the audience).

Brutus shows his idealism when he rejects the suggestion that they should swear an oath of allegiance. He has taken command of the situation now, and Cassius meekly accepts his decision to leave Cicero out of the conspiracy. He is more doubtful when Brutus—still idealistic—declares that Antony shall not be killed with Caesar, but he again allows himself to be overruled. The striking clock brings to an end the serious business of the meeting, and after a joke at the expense of Caesar, the conspirators leave Brutus to his thoughts.

Portia makes us remember the mental anguish that Brutus has endured. She is a character with whom we can sympathize, in her loving care for her husband, and whom we are intended to admire for her fortitude in bearing the wound in her thigh. Because of our feelings for Portia, we are sympathetic to the man she loves. There is no need, however, for the audience to hear what Brutus tells Portia about the conspiracy, so Shakespeare is able to show us a further example of the high regard in which the Romans hold Brutus. To Caius Ligarius, Brutus is a 'Brave son, deriv'd from honourable loins'; this is a final reminder of the nobility of Brutus, the man who can 'make sick men whole'.

Scene 2    Like Casca, Calphurnia is distressed by the unnatural events of the night, and she has also had a frightening dream, which Caesar narrates to Decius Brutus. But Decius is determined to get Caesar to the Capitol, and his interpretation of the dream is flattering. Tempted with the thought of a crown, and also afraid of being laughed at, Caesar has made up his mind to go out when the conspirators come to escort him.

Scene 3    Another warning has been prepared for Caesar. Artemidorus reads his letter aloud, so that we shall know what is in the paper that Caesar refuses to read.

Scene 4    Portia is anxious. Brutus has told her of the conspiracy, and she knows the danger that her husband is in. The tension grows.

## Act 3

Scene 1    Caesar, accompanied by the conspirators (like armed guards to see that he does not escape from them), approaches the Capitol. He rejects the petition from Artemidorus, and goes towards the Senate House, where the senators are waiting for him. Brutus and Cassius stay at the back of the procession. There is a moment of panic for Cassius, but Brutus calms him down; and now everything goes according to plan. At the very moment when Caesar is speaking of his own constancy (which reflects the order and constancy in the universe), chaos breaks loose. Caesar is killed; the conspirators (whom we now see as anarchists) proclaim the death of tyranny; 'Men, wives and children stare, cry out and run / As it were dooms-day'. Calphurnia's dream comes true when the conspirators, at Brutus's command, bathe their hands in Caesar's blood, congratulating themselves on having performed a deed which will be recorded in history.

Into this hysterical scene comes Antony's servant, calming the riot situation with his master's careful words, before Antony enters. At the beginning of this scene, Trebonius drew Antony aside, so that he did not go to the Capitol with Caesar; after the murder we hear that he has 'Fled to his house amaz'd'. Now he is very controlled. His speech to the conspirators sounds submissive, as though he were anxious to please them; but we ought not to ignore a possible irony in his address to them as 'gentlemen', nor a disgust in his reference to their 'purpled hands [that] do reek and smoke'. He is also perhaps ironic in describing them as 'The choice and master spirits of this age'—although we may not notice this until we read the play a second time, and know Antony's real feelings, which have not yet been made clear.

Antony shakes the hands of the murderers, taking note of their names; we remember that Brutus also shook the hands of the conspirators who came to his house, signifying his allegiance with them. Antony knows that he must be creating a bad impression that he is 'Either a coward or a flatterer'; but we must not be deceived by appearances. Brutus and Cassius contrast in their reception of Antony. Brutus welcomes him, sure that he will be a friend when he hears their explanations. Cassius, however, is still suspicious; he suggests a bribe, but he advises Brutus not to let Antony make the funeral oration. Once more, Brutus overrules Cassius.

Left alone on the stage, Antony shows that he is a loyal friend to Caesar—and a dangerous enemy to the conspirators. He prophesies the disasters that will follow Caesar's murder, and he has no sooner spoken than the first signs of impending war are apparent in the news that Octavius is coming to Rome. The movement of the play suddenly changes direction. Until now, everything has been aimed at the murder of Caesar; from this point, the aim is to secure revenge.

'Lend me your hand.' Antony asks the servant to help him carry Caesar's body off the stage. There were no curtains in the Elizabethan theatre, and competent dramatists ensured that after a murderous episode there were enough living characters on stage to remove the dead ones. Shakespeare was more than merely competent. Necessity demanded the introduction of another living character after Antony's prophetic speech, but Shakespeare makes a virtue out of necessity by having that character announce the coming of Octavius, so that the second movement of the play starts as soon as the first movement is completed.

Scene 2    The scene that follows invites us to make a contrast between two kinds of oratory, considered in terms of their effects on the citizens who hear the speeches. Brutus speaks in prose, trying to present a reasoned argument to justify the murder. The citizens are fairly satisfied with this, but it is ironic that they now wish to elevate Brutus into Caesar's place: they have not appreciated the principle behind Brutus's act. Antony's speech is in verse; there is no attempt to produce logical argument, for the oration—with its repetitions, rhetorical questions, ironies, and open display of emotion—is aimed at the hearts, and not the heads, of the people. We see the citizens in the process of changing their minds every time that Antony makes a well-calculated pause in his speech. Antony takes care with his references to the conspirators: his first allusion to them as 'honourable men' seems quite straightforward, but with each repetition the phrase gathers irony. It is a citizen, not Antony himself, who finally gives words to Antony's meaning: 'they were traitors. Honourable men!' Antony cannot be faulted for his understanding of the psychology of crowds, and he easily achieves his desired end.

Scene 3         The black comedy of this scene serves to lighten the tension that built up during and after Antony's oration. At the same time, the scene shows how the movement to avenge Caesar's murder is gathering force; in Act 4 it has erupted into civil war.

## Act 4

Scene 1         Passion has now given place to cold calculation as the members of the new triumvirate decide that in the coming 'purge' neither brother nor nephew shall be spared. Antony's dismissal of Lepidus —'a slight unmeritable man'—casts a suspicion of trouble to come; but Shakespeare is content to let the matter rest here.

Scene 2         More immediately serious is the lack of harmony between Brutus and Cassius, which must be kept secret from their armies.
Scene 3 Once again Brutus shows his idealism, which is outraged by Cassius' conduct. But Brutus has another cause for grief—his wife is dead.

Two passages in this scene duplicate the information about Portia's death. Shakespeare probably wrote first the version given in lines 180-94, and then—perhaps thinking that he had made Brutus too much a Stoic—added the lines that now appear as 145-55; and forgot to cross out the first draft. The play was not printed until 1623, and the printer would not tamper with an author's manuscript, even though the author was dead. So both versions were printed.

A decision has to be made by the conspirators whether to march to Philippi and encounter the Roman army there; or whether to remain in their present position. Cassius gives good reasons for staying where they are, but once more Brutus overrules him. This will prove fatal—as we are assured by the appearance of Caesar's ghost, with its ominous promise to Brutus: 'thou shalt see me at Philippi'.

## Act 5

In the scenes that follow, the absence of fixed scenery becomes a positive advantage, as the action moves from one camp to the other, located generally on the battlefield at Philippi. With our modern sound-effects, the noise of soldiers marching and fighting, coming nearer and moving further away, would make a good background for the speeches.

Scene 1   The armies of Brutus and Cassius have advanced towards Philippi, and Octavius' surprise confirms our suspicion that Brutus made the wrong decision. The verbal clash between Antony and Octavius, on one side, and Brutus and Cassius on the other, is in part a substitute for the physical combat impossible on stage. Antony and Octavius are victorious here—just as they will be in the real fighting.

Alone with Messala, Cassius loses the confidence with which he had answered Antony. Cassius has little hope left, and his parting with Brutus is very moving. It seems that Shakespeare is now working to increase our sympathies for the former conspirators.

Scene 2  
Scene 3   Now the fight has begun, and we hear from Brutus that things are going well with his soldiers. Cassius' army, however, has been overthrown, and a mistaken report of Brutus's situation causes him to despair. Defeated, he commits suicide. Titinius, finding the body, laments briefly; then kills himself, following Cassius' example in performing 'a Roman's part'. When Brutus comes upon the scene, he underlines the growing sense that Cassius was, after all, an honourable man and a true Roman: 'It is impossible that ever Rome / Should breed thy fellow'.

Scene 4   More skirmishes follow, and all the characters involved in them seem to be demonstrating their nobility: Young Cato dies bravely; Lucilius pretends to be Brutus in order to deceive the enemy soldiers; Antony is generous in his rescue and treatment of Lucilius.

Scene 5      But Brutus, in another part of the battlefield, recognizes that he is defeated. The friends that have gathered round him grieve, more for his sake than for their own; and Brutus rejoices in their loyalty when he finds that none of them will agree to his request and kill him. When at last he runs upon his sword, there is relief in his voice: 'Caesar now be still; / I kill'd not thee with half so good a will'.

     The conflict within Brutus—between love for Caesar and love for Rome—is at an end. His epitaph is spoken by Mark Antony, in terms that make us wonder whether Brutus, said to have been 'the noblest Roman of them all', was perhaps the true hero of Shakespeare's play, *Julius Caesar*.

# Brutus—'the noblest Roman of them all'?

The superlative praise of Antony's description of Brutus has a powerful effect on our minds, especially since it comes so close to the climax of the action, and only a few lines from the end of the play. We are left to wonder whether Brutus is, in fact, the hero of *Julius Caesar*—or whether Antony's obituary notice is speaking the whole truth.

Shakespeare takes the character of Brutus, with very little alteration, from *The Lives of the Greeks and Romans*, where Plutarch described him as

> a marvellous lowly and gentle person, noble minded, and would never be in any rage, nor carried away with pleasure and covetousness; but had ever an upright mind with him, and would never yield to any wrong or injustice.     (page 139)

In the play we begin to form a good opinion of Brutus from what the other characters say of him. Cassius is the first to speak his praises, but he assures Brutus (and us) that 'many of the best respect in Rome' (*1*, 2, 59) similarly esteem him. A glowing tribute to Brutus is expressed by Casca:

> O, he sits high in all the people's hearts,
> And that which would appear offence in us,
> His countenance, like richest alchemy,
> Will change to virtue and to worthiness.     (*1*, 3, 157–60)

From his mocking account of the ceremony with the crown (*1*, 2, 219 ff.) we have seen that Casca is not a man who is easily impressed; consequently we value his praise more highly.

When we see Brutus himself on the stage, we are conscious most of all of the mental anguish that he is suffering, torn between personal love for Caesar and patriotic love for Rome. He does not wish to worry Cassius, but prefers, as he says, to 'turn the trouble of my countenance / Merely upon myself' (*1*, 2, 38–9). It is very much in his favour that Brutus is not immediately won by Cassius' persuading but, having listened to the arguments, asks for time to consider them (*1*, 2, 163–9). His soliloquy in *Act 2*, scene 1 confirms our opinion of his sense of responsibility, and our sympathies are moved when he tells us that since Cassius first spoke to him (which

was four weeks earlier) he has not slept. Portia's account of his
distressed behaviour also makes us feel sympathetic towards her
husband, whilst Brutus's tenderness for his wife (and for the page
Lucius) is an attractive quality that we did not expect to find in
a man with so much on his mind.

We have no doubts about Caesar's love for Brutus, although
there is little time in the play for this to be demonstrated. It is
enough that we hear the famous cry '*Et tu, Brute*' when Caesar
discovers that his friend is one of the conspirators (3, 1, 77).
Plutarch told how Caesar gave up the fight for his life when he
recognized Brutus:

> Men report also that Caesar did still defend himself against
> the rest, running every way with his body. But when he saw
> Brutus with his sword drawn in his hand, then he pulled his
> gown over his head and made no more resistance.   (page 94)

We understand exactly what feelings were involved when Antony
explains to the crowd:

> Brutus, as you know, was Caesar's angel:
> Judge, O you gods, how dearly Caesar lov'd him.
> This was the most unkindest cut of all;
> For when the noble Caesar saw him stab,
> Ingratitude, more strong than traitors' arms,
> Quite vanquish'd him: then burst his mighty heart.
> 
> (3, 2, 182-7)

Brutus is always conscious of Caesar's love, and of the ingratitude with which he has repaid it. When he has been defeated, and
runs on his sword to avoid being captured, he seems to welcome
his death, almost as though it were a punishment for his offence in
killing Caesar: 'Caesar now be still; / I kill'd not thee with half so
good a will' (5, 4, 50-1). Yet the needs of Rome, as Brutus understands them, are more important than the demands of friendship
and in his speech to the Roman people Brutus offers justification
for his act: 'not that I loved Caesar less, but that I loved Rome
more' (3, 2, 22-3).

Brutus is an idealist. He is descended from patriots, and he is
often reminded of the Lucius Junius Brutus who drove Tarquin
from Rome and helped to found the first republic (see p. ix).
Brutus's motives for joining the conspiracy are wholly pure, and
he intends to maintain this purity in everything: to swear an oath
of allegiance between the conspirators would, he feels, 'stain / The
even virtue of our enterprise' (2, 1, 132-3), casting a shadow of

doubt both on the cause and on the men. He will not agree that
Antony should be killed along with Caesar, because this would turn
what he sees as ritual sacrifice into bloody butchery. Cassius argues
against Brutus here, and also when Antony asks permission to
address the citizens at Caesar's funeral. On both occasions Brutus's
idealism is strong, and Cassius is overruled; events prove Cassius
to have been right both times.

The contrast between the idealist, Brutus, and the realist,
Cassius, is never more clearly shown than in their quarrel about
money. The practical Cassius recognizes that, in time of war, 'it
is not meet / That every nice offence should bear his comment'
(4, 3, 7-8). Brutus, in a passion of honour, refuses to raise money
by ignoble means, and says he would 'rather coin my heart / And
drop my blood for drachmas' (4, 3, 72-3). We cannot help feeling
that this sentiment is very fine—but not much use for paying
soldiers.

The trouble with idealism is that it can so easily blind those
who possess it—and Brutus is blinded. The conspiracy *might* have
succeeded if Antony, as well as Caesar, had died on the ides of
March. All *might* still have been well for the murderers if Antony
had not been permitted to stir the citizens to mutiny with his funeral
oration. And there might even have been some little chance of
victory if Brutus had not insisted on marching to Philippi. But the
biggest mistake that Brutus makes is his initial decision, arrived
at with such difficulty, that Caesar has to die.

Brutus is wrong. It is easy to be influenced by a character so
sympathetically drawn as Brutus undoubtedly is, and to accept
that character's estimation of his own deeds. But when we read,
very carefully, the soliloquy in the garden, it becomes plain that
Brutus is deceiving himself. He confesses that he has 'no personal
cause' to fear Caesar and, furthermore, that he has never known
'when his affections sway'd / More than his reason' (2, 1, 11, 20-1).
Unable to fault Caesar from Caesar's own conduct, Brutus resorts
to a generalization, a 'common proof' (2, 1, 21), which says that
ambitious men, at the height of their power, scorn those beneath
them. With no more justification than this, Brutus argues that
Caesar is a potential tyrant and therefore must be killed. He himself admits that his argument is unacceptable—'Will bear no colour
for the thing he is'; and he attempts to rephrase it ('Fashion it
thus') in a more convincing manner (2, 1, 29-30). He convinces
himself—and patriotism does the rest.

It is patriotism, very largely, that leads Brutus into the trap
laid for him by Cassius. Caesar shows shrewd judgement when he

recognizes Cassius as one of those men who are 'never at heart's
ease / Whiles they behold a greater than themselves' (*1*, 2, 207–8).
Brutus is too innocent to see the danger that Caesar sees in Cassius,
but Cassius himself admits it to the audience when he gloats over
his success in manipulating the 'honourable mettle' of Brutus, so
that it is perverted from its true nature—'wrought / From that
it is dispos'd' (*1*, 2, 309–10).

The tragedy of Brutus lies here—not that he attempted to free
the republic of Rome from a tyrannous dictator and was killed in
the action; but that, *with the best of motives*, he was responsible
for the murder of

> the noblest man
> That ever lived in the tide of times.                    (*3*, 1, 256–7)

# Characters in the play

**Julius Caesar**

**Octavius Caesar**
**Mark Antony**          *triumvirs after the death of Julius Caesar*
**Aemilius Lepidus**

**Cicero**
**Publius**              *senators*
**Popilius Lena**

**Marcus Brutus**
**Cassius**
**Casca**
**Trebonius**
**Ligarius**             *conspirators against Julius Caesar*
**Decius Brutus**
**Metellus Cimber**
**Cinna**

**Flavius**
**Marullus**             *tribunes*
**Artemidorus**          *a schoolmaster*
**Cinna**                *a poet*

**Lucilius**
**Titinius**
**Messala**      *friends of Brutus and of Cassius*
**Young Cato**
**Volumnius**

**Varro**
**Clitus**
**Claudius**
**Strato**
**Lucius**      *servants or officers attending Brutus*
**Dardanius**
**Flavius**
**Labeo**

**Pindarus**      *servant to Cassius*

**Calphurnia**      *Caesar's wife*

**Portia**      *Brutus's wife*

A Soothsayer
Another Poet
Senators, Citizens, Attendants, Soldiers

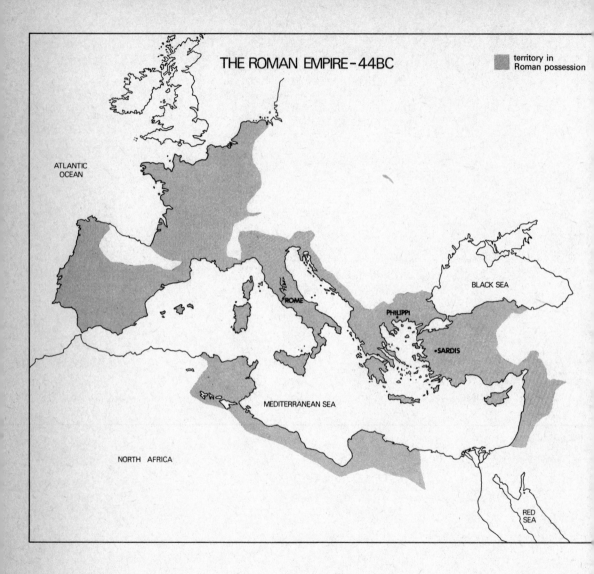

THE ROMAN EMPIRE – 44BC

territory in
Roman possession

ATLANTIC
OCEAN

BLACK SEA

ROME

PHILIPPI

SARDIS

MEDITERRANEAN SEA

NORTH AFRICA

RED
SEA

# Act I

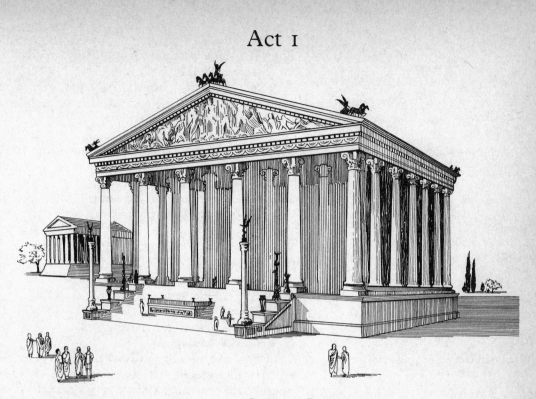

**Act I  Scene I**

The people of Rome are celebrating
a holiday in honour of Julius Caesar,
but Flavius and Marullus, their
tribunes (see p. ix), are angry. They
reproach the citizens because they have
forgotten their former ruler, Pompey;
and they fear that Caesar will prove to
be a tyrant when he alone is ruler of
Rome.

*mechanical :* manual workers.
*you . . . profession.* On a working
day, they should be equipped for work.


*rule :* ruler.


*in respect of :* in comparison with.
*cobbler :* both 'shoemaker' and
'poor workman'.

**Scene I** *Rome : a street*

> *Enter* Flavius, Marullus, *and some*
> Citizens

**Flavius**
Hence! home, you idle creatures, get you home.
Is this a holiday? What, know you not,
Being mechanical, you ought not walk
Upon a labouring day without the sign
5 Of your profession? Speak, what trade art thou?
  **First Citizen**
Why, sir, a carpenter.
  **Marullus**
Where is thy leather apron, and thy rule?
What dost thou with thy best apparel on?
You, sir, what trade are you?
  **Second Citizen**
10 Truly, sir, in respect of a fine workman, I am but,
as you would say, a cobbler.

**Marullus**

But what trade art thou? Answer me directly.

**Second Citizen**

A trade, sir, that I hope I may use with a safe
conscience; which is, indeed, sir, a mender of
15 bad soles.

**Marullus**

What trade, thou knave? thou naughty knave,
what trade?

**Second Citizen**

Nay, I beseech you, sir, be not out with me: yet
if you be out, sir, I can mend you.

**Marullus**

20 What meanest thou by that? Mend me, thou saucy
fellow!

**Second Citizen**

Why, sir, cobble you.

**Flavius**

Thou art a cobbler, art thou?

**Second Citizen**

Truly, sir, all that I live by is with the awl: I meddle
25 with no tradesman's matters, nor women's matters,
but withal I am, indeed, sir, a surgeon to old shoes;
when they are in great danger, I recover them. As
proper men as ever trod upon neat's leather have
gone upon my handiwork.

**Flavius**

30 But wherefore art not in thy shop today?
Why dost thou lead these men about the streets?

**Second Citizen**

Truly, sir, to wear out their shoes, to get myself
into more work. But indeed, sir, we make holiday
to see Caesar, and to rejoice in his triumph.

**Marullus**

35 Wherefore rejoice? What conquest brings he
home?
What tributaries follow him to Rome,
To grace in captive bonds his chariot wheels?
You blocks, you stones, you worse than senseless
things!
O you hard hearts, you cruel men of Rome,

---

13      *use* : practise.

15      *soles* : both 'soles (of shoes)' and
'souls'.

16      *naughty* : good for nothing.

18      *be not out* : don't be angry.
19      *if you be out* : if your shoes are
worn out.
        *mend* : both 'patch your shoes'
and 'improve your character'.

24      *awl* : a tool for making holes in
leather; the pun is with 'all'.

27      *recover* : with a pun on 're-cover'.
28      *proper* : fine.
        *neat's leather* : hide (the skin of
a cow).

34      *triumph* : triumphal procession
(see p. ix).

36      *tributaries* : captured enemies,
paying tribute-money to Caesar (and
to Rome).
37      *grace . . . bonds* : paying homage
by appearing in chains.
38      *senseless things* : objects incapable
of feeling (e.g. stones).

44 *livelong day*: all day long.

46 And as soon as you caught sight of his chariot.

47 *made an universal shout*: all shouted at once.

49 *replication*: echo.

50 *concave shores*: banks which overhang the river (and echo the noise).

52 *cull out a holiday*: pick this day for a holiday.

54 *Pompey's blood*: the sons of Pompey (whose blood has been shed).

57 *intermit*: delay.

58 *needs must light*: will inevitably fall.

59 *for this fault*: to atone for this fault.

60 *sort*: class.

61-3 Shed your tears into the river Tiber, until the very lowest water floods to the level of the highest bank.

64 *whe'r*: whether.

 *basest mettle*: humble spirits; the pun with 'metal' is continued with 'guilt' ('gilt') in the next line.

 *mov'd*: affected.

66 *Capitol*: the temple of Jupiter on the Capitoline Hill, overlooking the Forum (see p. 1).

67 *Disrobe . . . ceremonies*: tear the decorations from the statues.

70 *feast of Lupercal*: 15 February was a feast day in honour of Lupercus, protector of flocks and herds, to ensure the animals' fertility in the spring.

72 *Caesar's trophies*: decorations (e.g. scarves, compare 1, 2, 281) placed on the statues in honour of Caesar.

 *I'll about*: I'll walk through the city.

73 *the vulgar*: the common people.

75-7 If we suppress the people's enthusiasm for Caesar, it will be like pulling feathers from a falcon's wing; it will make him fly only at a normal height ('pitch') instead of soaring out of sight (like a god) to keep men, like slaves, afraid of him.

40 Knew you not Pompey? Many a time and oft
Have you climb'd up to walls and battlements,
To towers and windows, yea, to chimney-tops,
Your infants in your arms, and there have sat
The livelong day, with patient expectation,
45 To see great Pompey pass the streets of Rome;
And when you saw his chariot but appear,
Have you not made an universal shout,
That Tiber trembled underneath her banks,
To hear the replication of your sounds
50 Made in her concave shores?
And do you now put on your best attire?
And do you now cull out a holiday?
And do you now strew flowers in his way,
That comes in triumph over Pompey's blood?
55 Be gone!
Run to your houses, fall upon your knees,
Pray to the gods to intermit the plague
That needs must light on this ingratitude.
  **Flavius**
Go, go, good countrymen, and for this fault
60 Assemble all the poor men of your sort;
Draw them to Tiber banks, and weep your tears
Into the channel, till the lowest stream
Do kiss the most exalted shores of all.
       [*Exeunt all the* Citizens
See whe'r their basest mettle be not mov'd;
65 They vanish tongue-tied in their guiltiness.
Go you down that way towards the Capitol;
This way will I. Disrobe the images
If you do find them deck'd with ceremonies.
  **Marullus**
May we do so?
70 You know it is the feast of Lupercal.
  **Flavius**
It is no matter; let no images
Be hung with Caesar's trophies. I'll about
And drive away the vulgar from the streets;
So do you too, where you perceive them thick.
75 These growing feathers pluck'd from Caesar's wing
Will make him fly an ordinary pitch,
Who else would soar above the view of men
And keep us all in servile fearfulness.  [*Exeunt*

**Act 1   Scene 2**

Caesar, with his wife Calphurnia, Mark
Antony, and other important Romans,
walk in procession across the stage.
Brutus and Cassius leave the procession,
and discuss their uneasiness at having
Caesar as their ruler. Cassius recalls
an occasion when Caesar showed
himself to be physically weak. From
time to time shouts of joy, in praise of
Caesar, can be heard offstage, coming
from the Forum, and Cassius points
out that Caesar is being treated as
though he were superhuman. He warns
Brutus that Rome will be in danger
from such a man, and Brutus promises
to think about his words. Caesar and
the procession return, but Caesar now
looks angry. He speaks to Antony,
telling him that he is suspicious of
Cassius; then the procession leaves the
stage. Casca stays behind, and tells
Brutus and Cassius how Caesar was
offered a crown; he refused the crown,
and then fell down in an epileptic fit.
Brutus, Cassius and Casca arrange
another meeting; finally Cassius, alone
on the stage, speaks aloud his plans to
provoke Brutus to take action against
Caesar. For Plutarch's account of the
events in this scene, see p. 95.

3    *Antonius :* Latin form of Antony.
4    *course.* On the feast of Lupercal
(see note to *1, 1, 70*) young men ran
through the city and touched spectators
with leather straps; as Caesar explains,
it was believed that women who could
not bear children would, by this means,
be cured of their infertility ('sterile
curse').
6    *speed :* haste.
11   *Set on :* proceed.
15   *press :* crowd.

17   *turn'd.* We find out later in the
scene (line 212) that Caesar is deaf in
one ear.

**Scene 2** *Rome : a public place*

> *Enter in procession* Caesar; Antony, *ready*
> *for the course ;* Calphurnia, Portia, Decius,
> Cicero, Brutus, Cassius, *and* Casca;
> *followed by a crowd of* Citizens, *and*
> *a* Soothsayer

**Caesar**
Calphurnia.
    **Casca**
               Peace, ho! Caesar speaks.
  **Caesar**                      Calphurnia.
    **Calphurnia**
Here, my lord.
    **Caesar**
Stand you directly in Antonius' way
When he doth run his course. Antonius.
    **Antony**
5 Caesar, my lord?
    **Caesar**
Forget not, in your speed, Antonius,
To touch Calphurnia; for our elders say,
The barren, touched in this holy chase,
Shake off their sterile curse.
    **Antony**             I shall remember:
10 When Caesar says 'Do this,' it is perform'd.
    **Caesar**
Set on; and leave no ceremony out.
    **Soothsayer**
Caesar!
    **Caesar**
Ha! Who calls?
    **Casca**
Bid every noise be still: peace yet again!
    **Caesar**
15 Who is it in the press that calls on me?
I hear a tongue, shriller than all the music,
Cry 'Caesar!' Speak; Caesar is turn'd to hear.

**Soothsayer**
Beware the ides of March.
**Caesar**                               What man is that?
**Brutus**
A soothsayer bids you beware the ides of March.
**Caesar**
20 Set him before me; let me see his face.
**Cassius**
Fellow, come from the throng; look upon Caesar.
**Caesar**
What say'st thou to me now? Speak once again.
**Soothsayer**
Beware the ides of March.
**Caesar**
He is a dreamer; let us leave him. Pass.
                [*Trumpets sound. Exeunt all except* Brutus
                                *and* Cassius
**Cassius**
25 Will you go see the order of the course?
**Brutus**
Not I.
**Cassius**
I pray you, do.
**Brutus**
I am not gamesome: I do lack some part
Of that quick spirit that is in Antony.
30 Let me not hinder, Cassius, your desires;
I'll leave you.
**Cassius**
Brutus, I do observe you now of late:
I have not from your eyes that gentleness
And show of love as I was wont to have.
35 You bear too stubborn and too strange a hand
Over your friend that loves you.
**Brutus**                               Cassius,
Be not deceiv'd: if I have veil'd my look,
I turn the trouble of my countenance
Merely upon myself. Vexed I am
40 Of late with passions of some difference,
Conceptions only proper to myself,
Which give some soil, perhaps, to my behaviours;

---

8   *ides of March:* 15 March.

25   *order of the course:* progress of the race.

28   *gamesome:* interested in sport.

32   *I ... late:* I have been watching you recently.

34   *show:* expression.
     *was wont:* am accustomed.

35   Cassius compares Brutus to a rider who is unfamiliar ('strange') with his horse and is strict ('stubborn') in handling it.

37–9   *if ... myself:* if I have frowned (and so hidden my true expression), the frowns have been solely ('merely') for myself.

40   *Of late:* recently.
     *passions of some difference:* conflicting emotions.

41–2   Thoughts which concern me alone, but which perhaps have a bad effect ('soil') on my conduct.

44    *be you one :* you are certainly one.
45-7    Don't think any more of my neglect of you than that I am troubled with my personal problems, and so forget to show my friendly feelings to other people.
48    *passion :* feelings.
49-50    And for this reason I have kept hidden in my heart some very important thoughts.

52-3    A man cannot see himself unless he is reflected in something (e.g. a mirror).

56    *turn :* reflect.

58    *shadow :* reflection.
59    *best respect :* highest importance.
60    *immortal.* Cassius is being ironic.
61    *this age's yoke :* the oppression of these times.
62    *had his eyes :* i.e. the eyes of one of the 'best respect', so that he could see himself as others see him.

69    *modestly :* without exaggeration.
      *discover :* reveal.
71    *jealous on :* suspicious of.
72    *laughter :* subject of jest, a laughing-stock.
72-4    If I were in the habit ('use') of cheapening my love by swearing affection for every new acquaintance who declares (protests) his affection for me.
75    *fawn on :* flatter.
76    *scandal :* slander.
77-8    *That . . . rout :* that when I've had a few drinks I proclaim myself to be friends with all sorts of common people ('rout' = mob).
78    *hold :* consider.

But let not therefore my good friends be griev'd—
Among which number, Cassius, be you one—
45 Nor construe any further my neglect,
Than that poor Brutus, with himself at war,
Forgets the shows of love to other men.
      **Cassius**
Then, Brutus, I have much mistook your passion
By means whereof this breast of mine hath buried
50 Thoughts of great value, worthy cogitations.
Tell me, good Brutus, can you see your face?
      **Brutus**
No, Cassius; for the eye sees not itself
But by reflection, by some other things.
      **Cassius**
'Tis just:
55 And it is very much lamented, Brutus,
That you have no such mirrors as will turn
Your hidden worthiness into your eye,
That you might see your shadow. I have heard,
Where many of the best respect in Rome—
60 Except immortal Caesar—speaking of Brutus,
And groaning underneath this age's yoke,
Have wish'd that noble Brutus had his eyes.
      **Brutus**
Into what dangers would you lead me, Cassius,
That you would have me seek into myself
65 For that which is not in me?
      **Cassius**
Therefore, good Brutus, be prepar'd to hear;
And, since you know you cannot see yourself
So well as by reflection, I, your glass,
Will modestly discover to yourself
70 That of yourself which you yet know not of.
And be not jealous on me, gentle Brutus:
Were I a common laughter, or did use
To stale with ordinary oaths my love
To every new protester; if you know
75 That I do fawn on men and hug them hard,
And after scandal them; or if you know
That I profess myself in banqueting
To all the rout, then hold me dangerous.
      [*Flourish of trumpets, and shout, offstage*

**Brutus**
What means this shouting? I do fear the people
80 Choose Caesar for their king.
　　**Cassius**　　　　　　　　　　Ay, do you fear it?
Then must I think you would not have it so.
**Brutus**
I would not, Cassius; yet I love him well.
But wherefore do you hold me here so long?
What is it that you would impart to me?
85 If it be aught toward the general good,
Set honour in one eye and death i' th' other,
And I will look on both indifferently;
For let the gods so speed me as I love
The name of honour more than I fear death.
**Cassius**
90 I know that virtue to be in you, Brutus,
As well as I do know your outward favour.
Well, honour is the subject of my story.
I cannot tell what you and other men
Think of this life; but, for my single self,
95 I had as lief not be, as live to be
In awe of such a thing as I myself.
I was born free as Caesar; so were you:
We both have fed as well, and we can both
Endure the winter's cold as well as he:
100 For once, upon a raw and gusty day,
The troubled Tiber chafing with her shores,
Caesar said to me, 'Dar'st thou, Cassius, now
Leap in with me into this angry flood,
And swim to yonder point?' Upon the word,
105 Accoutred as I was, I plunged in
And bade him follow; so indeed he did.
The torrent roar'd, and we did buffet it
With lusty sinews, throwing it aside
And stemming it with hearts of controversy;
110 But ere we could arrive the point propos'd,
Caesar cried, 'Help me, Cassius, or I sink!'
I, as Aeneas, our great ancestor,
Did from the flames of Troy upon his shoulder
The old Anchises bear, so from the waves of Tiber
115 Did I the tired Caesar. And this man
Is now become a god, and Cassius is
A wretched creature, and must bend his body

---

85 *toward* : concerning.
*general* : public.

87 *indifferently* : impartially.

88 *speed* : favour.

91 *favour* : appearance.

94 *for my single self* : personally.

95 *as lief not be* : rather not live.

96 *such . . . myself* : a man as I am.

101 *chafing . . . shores* : raging at the restraint of the shores.

102 *Dar'st thou* : do you dare?

104 *Upon the word* : as soon as he spoke.

105 *Accoutred* : fully dressed.

107 *buffet* : contend with.

109 *stemming* : thrusting against.
*hearts of controversy* : competitive spirits (they were competing against the tide and against each other).

112 *Aeneas* : the founder of Rome, and therefore the spiritual ancestor of all Romans. He was a Trojan who, when Troy was captured, escaped from the burning city carrying his father, Anchises, on his back.

117 *bend his body* : bow.

118   *carelessly* : casually.
120   *fit* : spasm of shivering.
      *mark* : notice.
122   The colour would have drained
      from Caesar's lips in his sickness, but
      Cassius turns the sense round in order
      to present Caesar as a coward.
123   *bend* : look.
124   *his* : its.
125-6 It was Caesar's eloquence, not
      his commandment, that made the
      Romans record his speeches; but
      Cassius now wishes to show him as
      a tyrant.
127   *Titinius* : one of Cassius's friends.
129   *temper* : constitution.
130-1 Get ahead of all in the race for
      power (majesty), and alone carry off
      the prize (the crown of palm-leaves
      given to a conqueror).
131   *general* : from all the people.

If Caesar carelessly but nod on him.
He had a fever when he was in Spain,
120 And when the fit was on him, I did mark
How he did shake; 'tis true, this god did shake;
His coward lips did from their colour fly,
And that same eye whose bend doth awe the world
Did lose his lustre; I did hear him groan;
125 Ay, and that tongue of his, that bade the Romans
Mark him and write his speeches in their books,
Alas! it cried, 'Give me some drink, Titinius',
As a sick girl. Ye gods, it doth amaze me,
A man of such a feeble temper should
130 So get the start of the majestic world,
And bear the palm alone.
                    [*Flourish of trumpets; a second shout*
**Brutus**              Another general shout!
I do believe that these applauses are
For some new honours that are heap'd on Caesar.
       **Cassius**
Why, man, he doth bestride the narrow world

35   *Colossus*: the statue of Apollo, more than 100 feet high, which was destroyed by an earthquake in 224 B.C.; tradition says that its legs spanned the harbour at Rhodes.

38–40   Men are in control of their fates at some time in their lives, and it is our own faults, not something pre-destined by the positions of the stars when we were born, that we are now servants (and not masters).

44   If you speak the two names, 'Brutus' sounds as good as 'Caesar'.

45–6   If you use them to invoke ('conjure') spirits, one name is as likely as the other (a) to raise devils; and (b) to rouse men of courage.

49   *Age*: Cassius addresses the present time.

50   *noble bloods*: valiant and honourable men.

51   *the great flood*. Classical mythology tells how Zeus determined to destroy the whole world because men were so sinful; only one man, Deucalion, and his wife Pyrrha, were saved.

52   *fam'd with*: made famous by.

54   That the wide streets of Rome held only one man.

55   *Rome*: 'Rome' was pronounced, and often spelled, 'Room'.

56   *but one only man*: just a single man.

58   *a Brutus once*. The present Brutus claimed to descend from Lucius Junius Brutus, who was instrumental in expelling the Tarquins from Rome in 510 B.C.; see p. ix.
   *brook'd*: tolerated.

59   *keep his state*: maintain his kingdom.

60   *easily*: readily.

61   *am nothing jealous*: do not doubt.

62   *work*: persuade.

65–6   For the moment—if I can ask you as a friend—I would rather not be urged any further.

69   *meet*: suitable.
   *high*: important.

135   Like a Colossus; and we petty men
Walk under his huge legs, and peep about
To find ourselves dishonourable graves.
Men at some time are masters of their fates:
The fault, dear Brutus, is not in our stars,
140   But in ourselves, that we are underlings.
Brutus and Caesar: what should be in that 'Caesar'?
Why should that name be sounded more than
   yours?
Write them together, yours is as fair a name;
Sound them, it doth become the mouth as well;
145   Weigh them, it is as heavy; conjure with 'em,
'Brutus' will start a spirit as soon as 'Caesar'.
Now in the names of all the gods at once,
Upon what meat doth this our Caesar feed,
That he is grown so great? Age, thou art sham'd!
150   Rome, thou hast lost the breed of noble bloods!
When went there by an age, since the great flood,
But it was fam'd with more than with one man?
When could they say, till now, that talk'd of Rome,
That her wide walks encompass'd but one man?
155   Now is it Rome indeed, and room enough,
When there is in it but one only man.
O, you and I have heard our fathers say,
There was a Brutus once that would have brook'd
Th' eternal devil to keep his state in Rome
160   As easily as a king.
   **Brutus**
That you do love me, I am nothing jealous;
What you would work me to, I have some aim;
How I have thought of this and of these times,
I shall recount hereafter; for this present,
165   I would not, so with love I might entreat you,
Be any further mov'd. What you have said
I will consider; what you have to say
I will with patience hear, and find a time
Both meet to hear and answer such high things.

170    *chew upon :* think about.

171-4    Brutus would prefer to be a
country peasant than call himself
a Roman citizen under the oppression
that is likely to arise in these days.

175-7    Cassius compares his words to
steel striking flint to light a fire; as yet
he has only got a 'show of fire'
(enthusiasm) from Brutus, and 'but
thus much' may conceal his disappoint-
ment.

177    *Train :* band of followers.

179    *after . . . fashion :* in his cynical
way—which is demonstrated in lines
219-83.

180    *worthy note :* what happened that
is worth noting.

183    *chidden :* scolded.

185    *Cicero :* a great Roman orator and
statesman.
*ferret :* a rat-like animal with red
eyes.

187    *cross'd in conference :* opposed in
debates (which were held in the
Capitol).

193    *Yond Cassius :* that Cassius over
there.

196    *well given :* well disposed (towards
Caesar).

198    If the name of Caesar were
likely to be afraid.

170    Till then, my noble friend, chew upon this:
Brutus had rather be a villager
Than to repute himself a son of Rome
Under these hard conditions as this time
Is like to lay upon us.

**Cassius**                                        I am glad
175    That my weak words have struck but thus much
show
Of fire from Brutus.

*Enter* Caesar *and his Train*

**Brutus**
The games are done and Caesar is returning.

**Cassius**
As they pass by, pluck Casca by the sleeve,
And he will, after his sour fashion, tell you
180    What hath proceeded worthy note today.

**Brutus**
I will do so. But, look you, Cassius,
The angry spot doth glow on Caesar's brow,
And all the rest look like a chidden train:
Calphurnia's cheek is pale, and Cicero
185    Looks with such ferret and such fiery eyes
As we have seen him in the Capitol,
Being cross'd in conference by some senators.

**Cassius**
Casca will tell us what the matter is.

**Caesar**
Antonius!

**Antony**
190    Caesar?

**Caesar**
Let me have men about me that are fat,
Sleek-headed men, and such as sleep a-nights.
Yond Cassius has a lean and hungry look;
He thinks too much: such men are dangerous.

**Antony**
195    Fear him not, Caesar, he's not dangerous;
He is a noble Roman, and well given.

**Caesar**
Would he were fatter! But I fear him not;
Yet if my name were liable to fear,
I do not know the man I should avoid

200     *spare :* bony.

201-2    *he looks . . . men :* he sees right through the things that men do (to their motives for doing them).

204     *sort :* way.

205-6    *scorn'd . . . smile :* despised any man who could be persuaded to smile.

207     *at heart's ease :* fully contented.

214     *would you :* do you want to.

215     *chanc'd :* happened.

216     *sad :* serious.

219-20    *being offered :* when it was offered.

220     *put it by :* pushed it away.

221     *fell a-shouting :* started to shout.

227     *marry :* by the Virgin Mary (a mild oath, no stronger than 'indeed').

229     *mine honest neighbours.* Casca is being ironic.

---

200 So soon as that spare Cassius. He reads much,
He is a great observer, and he looks
Quite through the deeds of men; he loves no plays,
As thou dost, Antony; he hears no music;
Seldom he smiles, and smiles in such a sort
205 As if he mock'd himself, and scorn'd his spirit
That could be mov'd to smile at any thing.
Such men as he be never at heart's ease
Whiles they behold a greater than themselves,
And therefore are they very dangerous.
210 I rather tell thee what is to be fear'd
Than what I fear, for always I am Caesar.
Come on my right hand, for this ear is deaf,
And tell me truly what thou think'st of him.

> [*Trumpets sound. Exeunt* Caesar *and his Train.* Casca *stays behind*

**Casca**

You pull'd me by the cloak; would you speak with me?

**Brutus**

215 Ay, Casca; tell us what hath chanc'd to-day,
That Caesar looks so sad.

**Casca**

Why, you were with him, were you not?

**Brutus**

I should not then ask Casca what had chanc'd.

**Casca**

Why, there was a crown offered him; and, being
220 offered him, he put it by with the back of his hand,
thus; and then the people fell a-shouting.

**Brutus**

What was the second noise for?

**Casca**

Why, for that too.

**Cassius**

They shouted thrice: what was the last cry for?

**Casca**

225 Why, for that too.

**Brutus**

Was the crown offered him thrice?

**Casca**

Ay, marry, was 't, and he put it by thrice, every
time gentler than other; and at every putting-by
mine honest neighbours shouted.

**Cassius**
230 Who offered him the crown?
**Casca**
Why, Antony.
**Brutus**
Tell us the manner of it, gentle Casca.
**Casca**
I can as well be hanged as tell the manner of it
it was mere foolery; I did not mark it. I saw Mark
235 Antony offer him a crown; yet 'twas not a crown
neither, 'twas one of these coronets; and, as I told
you, he put it by once; but, for all that, to my thinking, he would fain have had it. Then he offered it
to him again; then he put it by again; but, to my
240 thinking, he was very loath to lay his fingers off it.
And then he offered it the third time; he put it the
third time by; and still as he refused it the rabblement hooted and clapped their chopped hands
and threw up their sweaty night-caps, and uttered
245 such a deal of stinking breath because Caesar
refused the crown, that it had almost choked Caesar
for he swounded and fell down at it: and for mine
own part, I durst not laugh, for fear of opening my
lips and receiving the bad air.
**Cassius**
250 But soft, I pray you: what! did Caesar swound?
**Casca**
He fell down in the market-place, and foamed at
mouth, and was speechless.
**Brutus**
'Tis very like: he hath the falling-sickness.
**Cassius**
No, Caesar hath it not; but you, and I,
255 And honest Casca, we have the falling-sickness.
**Casca**
I know not what you mean by that; but I am sure
Caesar fell down. If the tag-rag people did not clap
him and hiss him, according as he pleased and
displeased them, as they use to do the players in
260 the theatre, I am no true man.
**Brutus**
What said he, when he came unto himself?

234 *I did not mark it :* I paid no attention.
237 *to my thinking :* in my opinion.
238 *fain :* gladly.
242 *still :* always. *rabblement :* mob.
243 *hooted :* shouted. *chopped :* chapped (rough with work, weather-beaten).
244 *night-caps :* soft caps, often worn by day as well as night.
247 *swounded :* fainted.
250 *But soft :* wait a minute.
251-2 Casca describes the symptoms of an attack of epilepsy ('the falling-sickness').
253 *like :* likely.
257 *tag-rag people :* ragged mob.
259 *use :* are accustomed.

264    *me.* This word is used to add emphasis and contempt; it implies 'then and there'.
     *ope :* open.
     *doublet :* tunic worn by Elizabethan men (see pp. viii and 16).

265    *An :* if.
     *man of any occupation :* a man of action, a soldier (or perhaps a working man, such as those to whom Caesar spoke).

266    *at a word :* at his word—done what he told me to do.

269    *amiss :* wrong.
     *their worships.* This is probably Casca's sarcasm, not a true report of what Caesar said.

272-3    *there's . . . them :* you can't take any notice of them.

278    *spoke Greek.* Plutarch says that Cicero was nicknamed 'the Grecian'.

280    *an :* if.

283    *it was Greek to me.* A catchphrase meaning 'I could make no sense of it'.

285    *put to silence :* i.e. executed.

288    *sup :* have supper.

289    *am promised forth :* have promised to eat out (i.e. away from home).

291    *your mind hold :* you have not changed your mind.

**Casca**

Marry, before he fell down, when he perceived the common herd was glad he refused the crown, he plucked me ope his doublet and offered them his
265 throat to cut. An I had been a man of any occupation, if I would not have taken him at a word, I would I might go to hell among the rogues. And so he fell. When he came to himself again, he said, if he had done or said any thing amiss, he desired
270 their worships to think it was his infirmity. Three or four wenches, where I stood, cried, 'Alas! good soul', and forgave him with all their hearts: but there's no heed to be taken of them; if Caesar had stabbed their mothers, they would have done no less.

**Brutus**
275 And after that he came, thus sad, away?

**Casca**
Ay.

**Cassius**
Did Cicero say any thing?

**Casca**
Ay, he spoke Greek.

**Cassius**
To what effect?

**Casca**
280 Nay, an I tell you that, I'll ne'er look you i' th' face again; but those that understood him smiled at one another and shook their heads; but, for mine own part, it was Greek to me. I could tell you more news too; Marullus and Flavius, for pulling scarfs
285 off Caesar's images, are put to silence. Fare you well. There was more foolery yet, if I could remember it.

**Cassius**
Will you sup with me tonight, Casca?

**Casca**
No, I am promised forth.

**Cassius**
290 Will you dine with me tomorrow?

**Casca**
Ay, if I be alive, and your mind hold, and your dinner worth the eating.

**Cassius**

Good; I will expect you.

**Casca**

Do so. Farewell, both.                    [*Exit*

**Brutus**

295 What a blunt fellow is this grown to be!

He was quick mettle when he went to school.

**Cassius**

So is he now in execution

Of any bold or noble enterprise,

However he puts on this tardy form.

300 This rudeness is a sauce to his good wit,

Which gives men stomach to digest his words

With better appetite.

**Brutus**

And so it is. For this time I will leave you.

Tomorrow, if you please to speak with me,

305 I will come home to you; or, if you will,

Come home to me, and I will wait for you.

**Cassius**

I will do so; till then, think of the world.

[*Exit* Brutus

Well, Brutus, thou art noble; yet, I see,

Thy honourable mettle may be wrought

310 From that it is dispos'd: therefore 'tis meet

That noble minds keep ever with their likes;

For who so firm that cannot be seduc'd?

Caesar doth bear me hard; but he loves Brutus.

If I were Brutus now, and he were Cassius,

315 He should not humour me. I will this night,

In several hands, in at his windows throw,

As if they came from several citizens,

Writings, all tending to the great opinion

That Rome holds of his name; wherein obscurely

320 Caesar's ambition shall be glanced at:

And after this, let Caesar seat him sure;

For we will shake him, or worse days endure.

[*Exit*

296    *quick mettle*: lively.

297    *execution*: the performance.

299    *However*: despite the fact that.
       *tardy form*: appearance of slow-
       wittedness.

300-2    This rough manner emphasizes
         his keen intelligence, just as a sauce
         brings out the flavour of the meat; it
         also makes it more digestible—men are
         stimulated to think about what he says.

303    *For this time*: for the moment.

304    *please*: wish.

305    *to you*: to your house.

307    *the world*: the state of affairs.

309    *mettle*: spirit; Cassius plays with
       the sound 'metal', saying that Brutus's
       spirit can be worked upon like metal
       and twisted out of its natural shape.

310-12    *'tis meet . . . seduc'd*: it is
         important that men with noble natures
         should always be with others of the
         same nobility, because no man is so
         strong that he cannot be tempted.

313    *bear me hard*: dislike me.

314-15    Now if I were Brutus, and Brutus
         were Cassius, he would not be able to
         work on me (as I am going to work on
         him).

315-20    Cassius will throw into Brutus's
         window some letters, written in
         different handwritings ('several hands'),
         as though they came from different
         citizens. All the letters will speak of
         the high esteem in which Brutus is
         held in Rome, and Caesar's ambition
         will be indirectly ('obscurely') hinted
         ('glanced') at.

321    *seat him sure*: make certain that
       his position is secure.

## Act 1   Scene 3

A terrible storm has broken out, and Casca tells Cicero of the unnatural sights he has seen. Casca fears that some unknown evil is about to happen, but Cicero is not convinced, and goes home. Cassius next appears, rejoicing in the storm. Like Casca, he believes that it foretells a dreadful event, and he explains to Casca that there is a plot to overthrow Caesar. With Cinna, the two discuss how to persuade Brutus to join in their conspiracy.

1    *even* : evening.
      *brought . . . home* : did you escort Caesar to his house?
3    *sway* : realm.
4    *unfirm* : unsteady.
6    *riv'd* : torn.
      *knotty* : knotted.
7    *ambitious* : i.e. the ocean seemed to want to overreach its bounds.
8    *exalted with* : raised up to.
10   *dropping fire* : raining down lightning and thunder-bolts.
11   *civil strife in heaven* : civil war between the gods.
12   *saucy* : insolent.
13   *Incenses* : angers (literally, 'fires').

18   *Not sensible of* : not feeling.

20   *Against* : beside.
21   *glaz'd* : glared.
22   *annoying* : injuring.
22-3 *drawn Upon a heap* : huddled into a group.
23   *ghastly* : looking like ghosts.

26   *the bird of night* : the owl.

28   *prodigies* : unnatural events.
29   *conjointly* : all together.

30   *reasons* : causes.
31   *portentous* : ominous.
32   *climate* : region.
      *that . . . upon* : at which they are directed.

## Scene 3   *Rome : a street*

> *Thunder and lightning. Enter, from opposite sides of the stage,* Casca, *with his sword drawn, and* Cicero

**Cicero**
Good even, Casca : brought you Caesar home?
Why are you breathless, and why stare you so?
**Casca**
Are not you mov'd, when all the sway of earth
Shakes like a thing unfirm? O Cicero!
5 I have seen tempests, when the scolding winds
Have riv'd the knotty oaks; and I have seen
Th' ambitious ocean swell and rage and foam,
To be exalted with the threat'ning clouds;
But never till tonight, never till now,
10 Did I go through a tempest dropping fire.
Either there is a civil strife in heaven,
Or else the world, too saucy with the gods,
Incenses them to send destruction.

**Cicero**
Why, saw you any thing more wonderful?
**Casca**
15 A common slave—you know him well by sight—
Held up his left hand, which did flame and burn
Like twenty torches join'd; and yet his hand,
Not sensible of fire, remain'd unscorch'd.
Besides—I have not since put up my sword—
20 Against the Capitol I met a lion,
Who glaz'd upon me, and went surly by,
Without annoying me. And there were drawn
Upon a heap, a hundred ghastly women,
Transformed with their fear, who swore they saw
25 Men all in fire walk up and down the streets.
And yesterday the bird of night did sit,
Even at noon-day, upon the market-place,
Hooting and shrieking. When these prodigies
Do so conjointly meet, let not men say
30 'These are their reasons, they are natural';
For, I believe, they are portentous things
Unto the climate that they point upon.

**Cicero**

Indeed, it is a strange-disposed time:
But men may construe things, after their fashion,
35  Clean from the purpose of the things themselves.
Comes Caesar to the Capitol tomorrow?

**Casca**

He doth; for he did bid Antonius
Send word to you he would be there tomorrow.

**Cicero**

Good-night then, Casca: this disturbed sky
40  Is not to walk in.

**Casca**                                        Farewell, Cicero.

[*Exit* Cicero

*Enter* Cassius

**Cassius**

Who's there?

**Casca**             A Roman.

**Cassius**                              Casca, by your voice.

**Casca**

Your ear is good. Cassius, what night is this!

**Cassius**

A very pleasing night to honest men.

**Casca**

Who ever knew the heavens menace so?

**Cassius**

45  Those that have known the earth so full of faults.
For my part, I have walk'd about the streets,
Submitting me unto the perilous night,
And, thus unbraced, Casca, as you see,
Have bar'd my bosom to the thunder-stone;
50  And, when the cross blue lightning seem'd to open
The breast of heaven, I did present myself
Even in the aim and very flash of it.

**Casca**

But wherefore did you so much tempt the heavens?
It is the part of men to fear and tremble
55  When the most mighty gods by tokens send
Such dreadful heralds to astonish us.

**Cassius**

You are dull, Casca, and those sparks of life
That should be in a Roman you do want,
Or else you use not. You look pale, and gaze,
60  And put on fear, and cast yourself in wonder,
To see the strange impatience of the heavens;

**33** *a strange-disposed time :* a time in which strange things are happening.

**34-5** Men may interpret things, to suit themselves ('after their fashion'), quite contrary to the real nature ('purpose') of the things.

**39** *sky :* weather.

**42** *what night :* what a night.

**47** *Submitting me :* exposing myself.

**48** *unbraced :* with doublet unfastened.

**49** *thunder-stone :* thunder-bolt.

**50** *cross :* zig-zag.

**52** *Even in the aim :* just where it was directed.

**54** *part :* duty.

**55** *tokens :* signs.

**56** *heralds :* omens, foretelling disaster.
*astonish :* dismay.

**57** *dull :* stupid.

**58** *want :* lack.

**59** *use not :* do not make use of them.

**61** *impatience :* restlessness.

64    Why birds and beasts depart from their usual natures.

65    *calculate*: prophesy; it was thought by the Elizabethans that some mystic power was given to the very young and the very old, and also to natural idiots ('fools').

66    *ordinance*: ordained behaviour.

67    *pre-formed faculties*: qualities with which they were born.

68    *monstrous quality*: unnatural behaviour.

69    *infus'd . . . spirits*: poured these powers into them.

71    About some unnatural state of affairs.

But if you would consider the true cause
Why all these fires, why all these gliding ghosts,
Why birds and beasts, from quality and kind,
65 Why old men, fools, and children calculate;
Why all these things change from their ordinance,
Their natures, and pre-formed faculties,
To monstrous quality—why, you shall find
That heaven hath infus'd them with these spirits
70 To make them instruments of fear and warning
Unto some monstrous state.

72-8  Cassius could name a man
[Caesar] who is as unnatural as the
night and its strange events—one who
is an ordinary man in his own deeds
('personal action') yet who has become
a monster (prodigy) as threatening as
the strange outbreaks ('eruptions').

Now could I, Casca, name to thee a man
Most like this dreadful night,
That thunders, lightens, opens graves, and roars
75  As doth the lion in the Capitol;
A man no mightier than thyself or me
In personal action, yet prodigious grown,
And fearful as these strange eruptions are.
    **Casca**
'Tis Caesar that you mean; is it not, Cassius?
    **Cassius**
80  Let it be who it is: for Romans now

81  *thews*: sinews.
*like to*: similar to.
82  *woe the while*: alas for these times.

Have thews and limbs like to their ancestors;
But, woe the while! our fathers' minds are dead,
And we are govern'd with our mothers' spirits;

84  *yoke and sufferance*: the
oppression that we bear, and the way
we bear it.
85-8  History had taught Rome to fear
dictators, and although the Romans
were prepared to let Caesar rule the
Roman Empire, they refused to give
him absolute power at home.

Our yoke and sufferance show us womanish.
    **Casca**
85  Indeed, they say the senators tomorrow
Mean to establish Caesar as a king;
And he shall wear his crown by sea and land,
In every place, save here in Italy.
    **Cassius**
I know where I will wear this dagger then;

91  *Therein*: in this respect—i.e. by
giving men power to kill themselves.

90  Cassius from bondage will deliver Cassius:
Therein, ye gods, you make the weak most strong;
Therein, ye gods, you tyrants do defeat:
Nor stony tower, nor walls of beaten brass,
Nor airless dungeon, nor strong links of iron,

95  Can confine a resolved spirit.
96  *worldly bars*: restrictions of this
world.
97  *dismiss*: free.

95  Can be retentive to the strength of spirit;
But life, being weary of these worldly bars,
Never lacks power to dismiss itself.
If I know this, know all the world besides,

99  *That . . . bear*: the tyranny as it
affects me.

That part of tyranny that I do bear
100  I can shake off at pleasure.                [*Thunder*
    **Casca**                                    So can I:

101  *bondman*: prisoner.
102  *cancel*: the legal term for
destroying a deed or bond.

So every bondman in his own hand bears
The power to cancel his captivity.
    **Cassius**
And why should Caesar be a tyrant then?
Poor man! I know he would not be a wolf
105  But that he sees the Romans are but sheep;

106  *were no lion*: would not be a lion.
*hinds*: deer (also 'slaves').

He were no lion, were not Romans hinds.
Those that with haste will make a mighty fire

108    *trash :* brushwood, twigs.
109    *offal :* chips of wood.
110    *base matter :* material from which the fire starts.
       *illuminate :* light up, add to the glory of.

115    *indifferent :* unimportant.

117    *fleering :* scornful.
       *Hold, my hand :* here, let's shake hands (as a token of unity).
118    *Be . . . griefs :* form a party (faction) to get these troubles put right (redressed).
119–20  I will join you, and be as much involved as anyone else.
121    *know you :* let me tell you.
       *mov'd :* persuaded.
122    *Some certain :* certain individuals.
124    Whose outcome will be both honourable and dangerous.
125    *by this :* by this time.
       *stay :* are waiting.
126    *Pompey's porch :* the front of the theatre built by Pompey in 55 B.C.
128    *complexion of the element :* condition of the sky.
129    *In favour's :* in appearance is.

131    *Stand close :* keep hidden.

132    *gait :* walk.

134    *find out :* look for.

135–6  *incorporate . . . attempts :* united with us in our undertaking.
136    *stay'd for :* waited for.
137    *on't :* of it.

Begin it with weak straws; what trash is Rome,
What rubbish, and what offal, when it serves
110 For the base matter to illuminate
So vile a thing as Caesar! But, O grief,
Where hast thou led me? I, perhaps, speak this
Before a willing bondman; then I know
My answer must be made: but I am arm'd,
115 And dangers are to me indifferent.
    **Casca**
You speak to Casca, and to such a man
That is no fleering tell-tale. Hold, my hand:
Be factious for redress of all these griefs,
And I will set this foot of mine as far
120 As who goes furthest.     **Cassius**     There's a bargain made.
Now know you, Casca, I have mov'd already
Some certain of the noblest-minded Romans
To undergo with me an enterprise
Of honourable-dangerous consequence;
125 And I do know by this they stay for me
In Pompey's porch: for now, this fearful night,
There is no stir, or walking in the streets;
And the complexion of the element
In favour's like the work we have in hand,
130 Most bloody, fiery, and most terrible.

    *Enter* Cinna
    **Casca**
Stand close awhile, for here comes one in haste.
    **Cassius**
'Tis Cinna; I do know him by his gait:
He is a friend. Cinna, where haste you so?
    **Cinna**
To find out you. Who's that? Metellus Cimber?
    **Cassius**
135 No, it is Casca; one incorporate
To our attempts. Am I not stay'd for, Cinna?
    **Cinna**
I am glad on 't. What a fearful night is this!
There's two or three of us have seen strange sights.
    **Cassius**
Am I not stay'd for? Tell me.
    **Cinna**     Yes, you are.

143   *praetor* : magistrate.
144   *Where . . . it* : where only Brutus
      will find it.
145   *set . . . wax* : fasten it with wax.
146   *old Brutus* : Junius Brutus (see
      note to 1, 2, 158).
      *all this done* : when all this has
      been done.
147   *Repair* : make your way.

150   *hie* : hurry.
151   *bestow* : distribute.

155–6  Next time we meet him he will be
       entirely on our side.

157   *sits high* : is highly esteemed.
158   *offence* : criminal.
159   *countenance* : approval.
      *alchemy* : the 'science' that tried
      to change base metals (such as lead
      and tin) into gold.

162   *conceited* : understood and
      expressed.
163   *ere* : before.

140  O Cassius, if you could
     But win the noble Brutus to our party—
            **Cassius**
     Be you content. Good Cinna, take this paper,
     And look you lay it in the praetor's chair,
     Where Brutus may but find it; and throw this
145  In at his window; set this up with wax
     Upon old Brutus' statue: all this done,
     Repair to Pompey's porch, where you shall find us.
     Is Decius Brutus and Trebonius there?
            **Cinna**
     All but Metellus Cimber; and he's gone
150  To seek you at your house. Well, I will hie,
     And so bestow these papers as you bade me.
            **Cassius**
     That done, repair to Pompey's theatre.
                                   [*Exit* Cinna
     Come, Casca, you and I will yet ere day
     See Brutus at his house: three parts of him
155  Is ours already, and the man entire
     Upon the next encounter yields him ours.
            **Casca**
     O, he sits high in all the people's hearts,
     And that which would appear offence in us,
     His countenance, like richest alchemy,
160  Will change to virtue and to worthiness.
            **Cassius**
     Him and his worth and our great need of him
     You have right well conceited. Let us go,
     For it is after midnight; and ere day
     We will awake him and be sure of him.    [*Exeunt*

# Act 2

## Act 2    Scene 1

Brutus cannot sleep, because he is worried about the plot to murder Caesar. He thinks aloud about Caesar's ambition, which may be dangerous to the State. His servant brings a letter, and Brutus reads it. The letter urges him to take action, and just as he has finished reading it he is interrupted by Cassius, who brings with him the rest of the conspirators. Brutus addresses them, trying to inspire them with his own noble spirit. Cassius wants to murder Mark Antony as well as Caesar, but Brutus restrains him. After the conspirators have left, Brutus's wife Portia comes to him and begs to know what is worrying her husband. Finally Ligarius visits Brutus; he is sick, but when he hears that Brutus has need of him he feels strong and well.

2    *by . . . stars :* from the positions of the stars (the sky is still clouded with the storm).

4    I wish I could sleep as soundly as Lucius.

7    *taper :* candle.

10    *It . . . death :* Rome cannot be set free except by Caesar's death.

11    *spurn at :* kick.

12    *the general :* the good of the whole state.
    *would be :* wants to be.

13    The question is, what effect would it [being crowned king] have on his character.

14-15    Snakes come out on a warm day, so one has to be careful where one walks.

15    *that :* if we do that.

## Scene 1    *Rome : Brutus's orchard*

*Enter* Brutus

**Brutus**

What, Lucius! ho!
I cannot, by the progress of the stars,
Give guess how near to day. Lucius, I say!
I would it were my fault to sleep so soundly.
5 When, Lucius, when? Awake, I say! what, Lucius!

*Enter* Lucius

**Lucius**

Call'd you, my lord?

**Brutus**

Get me a taper in my study, Lucius:
When it is lighted, come and call me here.

**Lucius**

I will, my lord.                          [*Exit*

**Brutus**

10 It must be by his death: and, for my part,
I know no personal cause to spurn at him,
But for the general. He would be crown'd:
How that might change his nature, there's the
    question:
It is the bright day that brings forth the adder,
15 And that craves wary walking. Crown him—that;

| | |
|---|---|
| 16 | Then, I agree, we give him power to harm us. |
| 17 | *at his will :* as he wishes. |
| 18-19 | Greatness is misused when the great man exercises his power without also showing mercy. |
| 20-1 | When his desires over-ruled his reason. |
| 21 | *common proof :* a well-known fact. |
| 22 | The ambitious man starts to climb to power by being humble. |
| 23 | When he is on the way up, he pays special attention to humility. |
| 24 | *upmost round :* top rung (of the ladder). |
| 26-7 | *scorning . . . ascend :* rejecting the humility with which he started. |
| 28-9 | There's no cause ('colour') to quarrel with him for what he is now. |
| 30 | *Fashion it thus :* look at it this way. |
| 30-1 | *that . . . extremities :* that his present nature, given increased power, would lead him into such and such excesses (of tyranny). |
| 33 | *as his kind :* according to its nature. |
| | *mischievous :* harmful. |
| 35 | *taper :* candle. |
| | *closet :* study. |
| 36 | *window :* window-sill. |
| | *flint :* i.e. to strike a light with. |
| 44 | *exhalations :* meteors (the unnatural storm is still raging). |
| 47 | *Shall Rome, etc.* As Brutus says in lines 49-50, he has read this sort of thing before. |

And then, I grant, we put a sting in him,
That at his will he may do danger with.
Th' abuse of greatness is when it disjoins
Remorse from power; and, to speak truth of Caesar,
20 I have not known when his affections sway'd
More than his reason. But 'tis a common proof,
That lowliness is young ambition's ladder,
Whereto the climber-upward turns his face;
But when he once attains the upmost round,
25 He then unto the ladder turns his back,
Looks in the clouds, scorning the base degrees
By which he did ascend. So Caesar may;
Then, lest he may, prevent. And, since the quarrel
Will bear no colour for the thing he is,
30 Fashion it thus: that what he is, augmented,
Would run to these and these extremities;
And therefore think him as a serpent's egg
Which, hatch'd, would, as his kind, grow
    mischievous,
And kill him in the shell.

*Enter* Lucius

**Lucius**
35 The taper burneth in your closet, sir.
Searching the window for a flint, I found
This paper, thus seal'd up; and I am sure
It did not lie there when I went to bed.
                                                    [*Gives him a letter*

**Brutus**
Get you to bed again; it is not day.
40 Is not tomorrow, boy, the ides of March?

**Lucius**
I know not, sir.

**Brutus**
Look in the calendar, and being me word.

**Lucius**
I will, sir.                                              [*Exit*

**Brutus**
The exhalations whizzing in the air
45 Give so much light that I may read by them.
                                                    [*Opens the letter*
*Brutus, thou sleep'st : awake and see thyself.*
*Shall Rome, etc. Speak, strike, redress!*

49   *instigations* : letters urging him to take action.

50   *took* : picked.

51   *piece it out* : fill in the gaps.

52   *under . . . awe* : in fear of one man.

53   *My ancestors.* See note to *1, 2, 158.*

56–8   Brutus promises that if things can be set right (redressed) as a result of his speaking and striking, then Rome shall be granted her whole request ('petition') by him.

59   *wasted fifteen days.* Lucius includes the day that is dawning in his reckoning of time that has passed ('wasted').

59sd   *within* : offstage.

61   *whet* : incite (a knife is 'whetted' when it is sharpened).

63–5   The interval ('interim') between the first impulse ('motion') to do a dreadful deed, and the performance ('acting') of the deed, is like a nightmare ('phantasma') or a horrid dream.

66–9   Brutus makes a familiar (to the Elizabethans) comparison between the nature of an individual man and an earthly kingdom. When the immortal spirit ('genius') argues (is 'in council') with the mortal faculties ('instruments'), man's nature is disturbed, just as a kingdom is disturbed by a civil war ('insurrection'). This is why Brutus cannot sleep.

70   *brother.* Cassius was married to Brutus's sister Junia.

73   *pluck'd about* : drawn down over.

75   *discover* : identify them.

---

'Brutus, thou sleep'st: awake'.
Such instigations have been often dropp'd
50  Where I have took them up.
'Shall Rome, etc.' Thus must I piece it out:
Shall Rome stand under one man's awe? What,
   Rome?
My ancestors did from the streets of Rome
The Tarquin drive, when he was call'd a king.
55  'Speak, strike, redress!' Am I entreated
To speak, and strike? O Rome, I make thee
   promise:
If the redress will follow, thou receivest
Thy full petition at the hand of Brutus!

*Enter* Lucius

**Lucius**
Sir, March is wasted fifteen days.
                           [*Knocking within*

**Brutus**
60  'Tis good. Go to the gate: somebody knocks.
                           [*Exit* Lucius
Since Cassius first did whet me against Caesar,
I have not slept.
Between the acting of a dreadful thing
And the first motion, all the interim is
65  Like a phantasma, or a hideous dream:
The genius and the mortal instruments
Are then in council; and the state of man,
Like to a little kingdom, suffers then
The nature of an insurrection.

*Enter* Lucius

**Lucius**
70  Sir, 'tis your brother Cassius at the door,
Who doth desire to see you.
**Brutus**                    Is he alone?
**Lucius**
No, sir, there are more with him.
**Brutus**             Do you know them?
**Lucius**
No, sir; their hats are pluck'd about their ears,
And half their faces buried in their cloaks,
75  That by no means I may discover them

76    *mark of favour* : feature.

77    *faction* : party of conspirators.

79    *free* : common.

83    *path . . . on* : walk around with your natural face.
84    *Erebus* : hell.
85    *prevention* : (being recognized and) stopped.

86    *bold upon* : presumptuous in interrupting.

88    *this hour* : for an hour.

98    *watchful* : that keep you awake.
98-9  *interpose . . . night* : prevent your eyes from closing.

100   *entreat a word.* Cassius must make sure, in private conversation, that Brutus is won over to the conspirators' side.

By any mark of favour.
**Brutus**                                    Let 'em enter
                                          [*Exit* Lucius
They are the faction. O conspiracy,
Sham'st thou to show thy dangerous brow by night
When evils are most free? O, then by day
80 Where wilt thou find a cavern dark enough
To mask thy monstrous visage? Seek none, con-
        spiracy;
Hide it in smiles and affability:
For if thou path, thy native semblance on,
Not Erebus itself were dim enough
85 To hide thee from prevention.

        *Enter the Conspirators*, Cassius, Casca,
        Decius, Cinna, Metellus Cimber, *and*
        Trebonius
**Cassius**
I think we are too bold upon your rest:
Good morrow, Brutus; do we trouble you?
**Brutus**
I have been up this hour, awake all night.
Know I these men that come along with you?
**Cassius**
90 Yes, every man of them; and no man here
But honours you; and every one doth wish
You had but that opinion of yourself
Which every noble Roman bears of you.
This is Trebonius.
**Brutus**                        He is welcome hither
**Cassius**
95 This, Decius Brutus.
**Brutus**                        He is welcome too
**Cassius**
This, Casca; this, Cinna;
And this, Metellus Cimber.
**Brutus**                        They are all welcome.
What watchful cares do interpose themselves
Betwixt your eyes and night?
**Cassius**
100 Shall I entreat a word?
                        [Brutus *and* Cassius *whisper*
**Decius**
Here lies the east: doth not the day break here?

104   *fret :* streak.

106-11   *as I point my sword.* Casca points his sword towards the Capitol (line 111), where Caesar will be murdered. It is much more ('a great way growing') towards the south than the direction in which Cinna and Decius Brutus are looking. Perhaps he is right to say that because it is spring ('Weighing the youthful season of the year') they must look in this direction to see the early sun. But the dawn of the revolution, heralded by Caesar's death, is really in his mind.

112   *all over :* all of you.

113   *swear :* Cassius perhaps interprets 'Give me your hands all over' as a suggestion that the conspirators should all lay their hands on the hilt of a sword and swear by that to keep faith.

114-16   *if not . . . betimes :* if the evils that show their effects in men's faces, our own mental pain, and the corruption of the age, are not strong enough motives, we ought to give up at once ('betimes').

117   *idle bed :* bed of idleness.

118   *high-sighted tyranny :* tyranny that looks down from a great height.
        *range on :* roam at large (like a beast in search of prey).

119   *by lottery :* by chance (at the tyrant's whim).
        *these :* i.e. the conspirators.

120   *bear fire :* are spirited.

121   *kindle :* set aflame.

124   *prick :* urge.
        *redress :* put things right.

125   *secret :* trustworthy.
        *spoke the word :* given our promise.

126   *palter :* cheat.

127   *honesty to honesty :* one honest man to another.
        *engag'd :* promised.

128   *this . . . it :* we will succeed or die.

129   *Swear priests :* let priests swear.
        *cautelous :* deceiving.

**Casca**

No.

**Cinna**

O, pardon, sir, it doth; and yon grey lines
That fret the clouds are messengers of day.

**Casca**

105   You shall confess that you are both deceiv'd.
Here, as I point my sword, the sun arises;
Which is a great way growing on the south,
Weighing the youthful season of the year.
Some two months hence, up higher toward the north

110   He first presents his fire; and the high east
Stands, as the Capitol, directly here.

**Brutus**

Give me your hands all over, one by one.

**Cassius**

And let us swear our resolution.

**Brutus**

No, not an oath: if not the face of men,

115   The sufferance of our souls, the time's abuse—
If these be motives weak, break off betimes,
And every man hence to his idle bed;
So let high-sighted tyranny range on,
Till each man drop by lottery. But if these,

120   As I am sure they do, bear fire enough
To kindle cowards and to steel with valour
The melting spirits of women, then, countrymen,
What need we any spur but our own cause
To prick us to redress? what other bond

125   Than secret Romans, that have spoke the word
And will not palter? and what other oath
Than honesty to honesty engag'd,
That this shall be, or we will fall for it?
Swear priests and cowards and men cautelous,

130    *carrions :* (men who are no better than) corpses.

130-1    *such . . . wrongs :* men who are so patient that they seem to be glad when they are injured.

131-2    *unto . . . doubt :* men who are not to be trusted swear oaths to commit crimes.

133    *even :* total.

134    *insuppressive :* undaunted.

135    *or . . . or :* either . . . or.

136-8    *when . . . bastardy :* when every drop of blood in each of us will be guilty of not being true Roman blood.

140    *that . . . him :* that he has given.

141    *sound him :* find out what he thinks.

142    *stand . . . us :* support us strongly.

144    *silver hairs.* The metaphor is carried on in the next two lines.

148    *no whit :* not at all.

150    *break with :* confide in.

155    *well urg'd :* a good idea.
        *meet :* fitting.

157    *of him :* in him.

158    *shrewd :* keen.
        *contriver :* plotter.
        *means :* resources.

159    *improve :* make the most of.

160    *annoy :* injure.

162    *course :* course of action.

164    As though we were angry when we killed him, but showed personal malice after he was dead.

130  Old feeble carrions and such suffering souls
     That welcome wrongs; unto bad causes swear
     Such creatures as men doubt; but do not stain
     The even virtue of our enterprise,
     Nor th' insuppressive mettle of our spirits,
135  To think that or our cause or our performance
     Did need an oath; when every drop of blood
     That every Roman bears, and nobly bears,
     Is guilty of a several bastardy,
     If he do break the smallest particle
140  Of any promise that hath pass'd from him.
        **Cassius**
     But what of Cicero? Shall we sound him?
     I think he will stand very strong with us.
        **Casca**
     Let us not leave him out.
        **Cinna**                    No, by no means.
        **Metellus**
     O, let us have him; for his silver hairs
145  Will purchase us a good opinion,
     And buy men's voices to commend our deeds:
     It shall be said his judgment rul'd our hands;
     Our youths and wildness shall no whit appear,
     But all be buried in his gravity.
        **Brutus**
150  O name him not: let us not break with him;
     For he will never follow any thing
     That other men begin.
        **Cassius**                  Then leave him out.
        **Casca**
     Indeed he is not fit.
        **Decius**
     Shall no man else be touch'd but only Caesar?
        **Cassius**
155  Decius, well urg'd. I think it is not meet,
     Mark Antony, so well belov'd of Caesar,
     Should outlive Caesar: we shall find of him
     A shrewd contriver; and, you know, his means,
     If he improve them, may well stretch so far
160  As to annoy us all; which to prevent,
     Let Antony and Caesar fall together.
        **Brutus**
     Our course will seem too bloody, Caius Cassius,
     To cut the head off and then hack the limbs,
     Like wrath in death and envy afterwards;

165 For Antony is but a limb of Caesar.
Let us be sacrificers, but not butchers, Caius.
We all stand up against the spirit of Caesar;
And in the spirit of men there is no blood:
O, then that we could come by Caesar's spirit,
170 And not dismember Caesar! But, alas,
Caesar must bleed for it. And, gentle friends,
Let's kill him boldly, but not wrathfully;
Let's carve him as a dish fit for the gods,
Not hew him as a carcass fit for hounds:
175 And let our hearts, as subtle masters do,
Stir up their servants to an act of rage,
And after seem to chide 'em. This shall make
Our purpose necessary, and not envious;
Which so appearing to the common eyes,
180 We shall be call'd purgers, not murderers.
And, for Mark Antony, think not of him;
For he can do no more than Caesar's arm
When Caesar's head is off.

**Cassius**                         Yet I fear him;
For in the ingrafted love he bears to Caesar—

**Brutus**

185 Alas, good Cassius, do not think of him.
If he love Caesar, all that he can do
Is to himself, take thought and die for Caesar:
And that were much he should; for he is given
To sports, to wildness, and much company.

**Trebonius**

190 There is no fear in him; let him not die,
For he will live, and laugh at this hereafter.

**Brutus**                         [Clock strikes
Peace! count the clock.

**Cassius**                  The clock hath stricken three.

**Trebonius**
'Tis time to part.

**Cassius**                  But it is doubtful yet
Whether Caesar will come forth today or no;
195 For he is superstitious grown of late,
Quite from the main opinion he held once
Of fantasy, of dreams, and ceremonies.
It may be, these apparent prodigies,
The unaccustom'd terror of this night,
200 And the persuasion of his augurers,
May hold him from the Capitol today.

---

67  We are rebelling against what Caesar represents (i.e. tyranny).

69  *come by*: take possession of.

75  *subtle*: crafty.
76  *Stir up*: incite.
78  *purpose*: action.
    *necessary*: i.e. for the good of the State.
    *envious*: malicious.
79  When it looks like this in the eyes of the people.
80  *purgers*: surgeons (who treated patients by drawing off—purging—infected blood).

84  *ingrafted*: deeply rooted.

87  *to himself*: against himself.
    *take thought*: take it to heart.
88  *that . . . should*: that is too much to ask from him.

90  *no fear in*: nothing to fear from.

95  For he has recently become superstitious.
96  *Quite*: very different.
    *main*: strong.
97  *ceremonies*: ritual prediction of the future.
98  *apparent prodigies*: wonders that have appeared.
00  *augurers*: soothsayers, priests who interpreted the omens.
01  *hold*: keep.

203      *o'ersway him :* make him change
his mind.

204-5   *unicorns . . . holes.* According to
legend, a hunter stood behind a tree
when he was charged by a unicorn
(a mythical beast). He then dodged
out at the last moment, and the unicorn
drove its horn into the trunk of the
tree, and was held fast. It was also
thought that bears could easily be
caught after they had been confused
by seeing their own reflections in
mirrors ('glasses'); and that in order to
trap an elephant, the hunter would
dig a pit, and hide the hole with
branches, so that the elephant would
fall into it.

206      *toils :* snares.

210      I can turn his mood in the right
way.

213      *uttermost :* latest time.

215      *bear Caesar hard :* hate Caesar.

216      *rated :* reproved.

218      *by him :* by way of his house.

219      *reasons :* i.e. for mistrusting
Caesar.

220      *fashion him :* persuade him to
join us.

225      *put on :* take on the same
appearance as.

226      *bear it :* carry it off.

227      *untir'd :* unflagging.
*formal constancy :* usual dignified
behaviour.

230      *honey . . . slumber :* sleep which
is sweet ('honey'), deep ('heavy'), and
as refreshing as the dew.

231      *figures :* problems.
*fantasies :* imaginings.

232      *busy :* restless.
*draws :* creates.

**Decius**
Never fear that : if he be so resolv'd,
I can o'ersway him ; for he loves to hear
That unicorns may be betray'd with trees,
205  And bears with glasses, elephants with holes,
Lions with toils, and men with flatterers ;
But when I tell him he hates flatterers,
He says he does, being then most flattered.
Let me work ;
210  For I can give his humour the true bent,
And I will bring him to the Capitol.
    **Cassius**
Nay, we will all of us be there to fetch him.
    **Brutus**
By the eighth hour : is that the uttermost ?
    **Cinna**
Be that the uttermost, and fail not then.
    **Metellus**
215  Caius Ligarius doth bear Caesar hard,
Who rated him for speaking well of Pompey :
I wonder none of you have thought of him.
    **Brutus**
Now, good Metellus, go along by him :
He loves me well, and I have given him reasons ;
220  Send him but hither, and I'll fashion him.
    **Cassius**
The morning comes upon's ; we'll leave you, Brutus.
And, friends, disperse yourselves ; but all remember
What you have said, and show yourselves true
    Romans.
    **Brutus**
Good gentlemen, look fresh and merrily ;
225  Let not our looks put on our purposes,
But bear it as our Roman actors do,
With untir'd spirits and formal constancy.
And so good morrow to you every one.
                              [*Exeunt all except* Brutus
Boy ! Lucius ! Fast asleep ? It is no matter ;
230  Enjoy the honey-heavy dew of slumber :
Thou hast no figures nor no fantasies
Which busy care draws in the brains of men ;
Therefore thou sleep'st so sound.

*Enter* Portia

**Portia**                                    Brutus, my lord!

**Brutus**

Portia, what mean you? Wherefore rise you now?

235 It is not for your health thus to commit
Your weak condition to the raw cold morning.

**Portia**

Nor for yours neither. Y'have ungently, Brutus,
Stole from my bed; and yesternight at supper
You suddenly arose, and walk'd about,

240 Musing and sighing, with your arms across,
And when I ask'd you what the matter was,
You star'd upon me with ungentle looks.
I urg'd you further; then you scratch'd your head,
And too impatiently stamp'd with your foot;

245 Yet I insisted, yet you answer'd not,
But, with an angry wafture of your hand,
Gave sign for me to leave you. So I did,
Fearing to strengthen that impatience
Which seem'd too much enkindled, and withal

250 Hoping it was but an effect of humour,
Which sometime hath his hour with every man.
It will not let you eat, nor talk, nor sleep;
And could it work so much upon your shape
As it hath much prevail'd on your condition,

255 I should not know you Brutus. Dear my lord,
Make me acquainted with your cause of grief.

**Brutus**

I am not well in health, and that is all.

**Portia**

Brutus is wise, and were he not in health,
He would embrace the means to come by it.

**Brutus**

260 Why, so I do. Good Portia, go to bed.

**Portia**

Is Brutus sick, and is it physical
To walk unbraced and suck up the humours
Of the dank morning? What, is Brutus sick,
And will he steal out of his wholesome bed

265 To dare the vile contagion of the night,
And tempt the rheumy and unpurged air
To add unto his sickness? No, my Brutus;
You have some sick offence within your mind,

---

34    *what mean you :* what do you want?

35    *not for :* not good for.
      *commit :* expose.

36    *weak condition :* delicate health.

37    *ungently :* unkindly.

40    *across :* folded.

45    *Yet :* still.

46    *wafture :* wave.

49    *enkindled :* provoked.
      *withal :* also.

50    *an effect of humour :* caused by some passing mood.

51    Which affects everybody from time to time.

53-5  And if it could alter your appearance as much as it has changed your state of mind, I should not recognize you as Brutus.

56    *your cause of grief :* the cause of your grief.

59    He would follow some course to gain health.

61    *physical :* medicinal.

62    *unbraced :* with doublet unfastened.
      *suck up :* breathe in.
      *humours :* dampness.

63    *dank :* cold and damp.

65    To risk catching some horrible infection carried on the night air.

66    *rheumy . . . air :* air that has not yet been purified (purged) by the sun, and will give you catarrh.

68    *sick offence :* sorrow that makes you sick.

269     *by . . . place :* because I am your wife.

271     *charm :* implore.
        *by . . . beauty.* Portia tries to use her beauty to bewitch Brutus.

272     *that great vow :* i.e. the marriage vow.

273     Which did unite us into one flesh.

274     *unfold :* disclose.

275     *heavy :* solemn.

276     *had resort :* visited.

278     *Even from darkness :* although it was dark.

280-3   *bond of marriage.* The legal language is continued in '*Is it excepted*' (= is there some exception in the agreement); '*appertain*' (= belong); '*sort*' (= a particular manner); '*limitation*' (= for a limited period of time).

284     *keep with :* accompany.

285     *suburbs :* outskirts; in Elizabethan London the brothels were situated in the suburbs, and this leads to Portia's conclusion in line 287.

289     *drops :* i.e. of blood.

290     *visit.* The Elizabethans thought that blood was made in the liver, and flowed from there to the heart.

292     *grant :* admit.
        *withal :* in spite of that.

293     *took to wife :* married.

295     *well-reputed :* of good reputation.
        *Cato.* Portia's father was esteemed for his integrity, courage, and high principles. He fought for Pompey in the civil war, and killed himself to avoid being captured by Caesar.

296     *my sex :* other women.

297     Having such a father and such a husband.

298     *counsels :* plans.

299     *strong proof :* a severe test.
        *constancy :* endurance.

Which, by the right and virtue of my place,
270 I ought to know of; and, upon my knees,
                                    [*She kneels*
I charm you, by my once-commended beauty,
By all your vows of love, and that great vow
Which did incorporate and make us one,
That you unfold to me, your self, your half,
275 Why you are heavy, and what men tonight
Have had resort to you; for here have been
Some six or seven, who did hide their faces
Even from darkness.

**Brutus**                    Kneel not, gentle Portia
**Portia**
I should not need, if you were gentle Brutus.
280 Within the bond of marriage, tell me, Brutus,
Is it excepted, I should know no secrets
That appertain to you? Am I your self
But, as it were, in sort or limitation,
To keep with you at meals, comfort your bed,
285 And talk to you sometimes? Dwell I but in the suburbs
Of your good pleasure? If it be no more,
Portia is Brutus' harlot, not his wife.

**Brutus**
You are my true and honourable wife,
As dear to me as are the ruddy drops
290 That visit my sad heart.

**Portia**
If this were true, then should I know this secret.
I grant I am a woman, but, withal,
A woman that Lord Brutus took to wife;
I grant I am a woman, but, withal,
295 A woman well-reputed, Cato's daughter.
Think you I am no stronger than my sex,
Being so father'd and so husbanded?
Tell me your counsels, I will not disclose 'em.
I have made strong proof of my constancy.
300 Giving myself a voluntary wound
Here, in the thigh: can I bear that with patience
And not my husband's secrets?

**Brutus**                         O ye gods!
Render me worthy of this noble wife.

                                    [*Knocking within*

| | | |
|---|---|---|
| 305 | *bosom* : heart. | |
| | *partake* : share. | |
| 307 | *engagements* : commitments. | |
| | *construe* : explain. | |
| 308 | All that is written (charactered) on my forehead—i.e. the meaning of the worried lines. | |

Hark, hark! one knocks. Portia, go in awhile;
305 And by and by thy bosom shall partake
The secrets of my heart.
All my engagements I will construe to thee,
All the charactery of my sad brows.
Leave me with haste.                    [*Exit* Portia
Lucius, who's that knocks?

*Enter* Lucius *with* Ligarius

**Lucius**
310 Here is a sick man that would speak with you.

**Brutus**
Caius Ligarius, that Metellus spoke of.
Boy, stand aside. Caius Ligarius, how?

312  *how* : how are you?

**Ligarius**
Vouchsafe good morrow from a feeble tongue.

313  *Vouchsafe* : may I say.

**Brutus**
O what a time have you chose out, brave Caius,
315 To wear a kerchief! Would you were not sick.

315  *kerchief* : scarf—i.e. to be ill.

**Ligarius**
I am not sick if Brutus have in hand
Any exploit worthy the name of honour.

**Brutus**
Such an exploit have I in hand, Ligarius,
Had you a healthful ear to hear of it.

319  If you were well enough to hear it.

**Ligarius**
320 By all the gods that Romans bow before
I here discard my sickness. Soul of Rome!
Brave son, deriv'd from honourable loins!
Thou, like an exorcist, hast conjur'd up
My mortified spirit. Now bid me run,
325 And I will strive with things impossible;
Yea, get the better of them. What's to do?

322  *deriv'd* : descended.
     *loins* : i.e. ancestors.
323  *exorcist* : one who controls spirits by his magical commandments (conjuring).
324  *mortified* : dead.
325  I will try to do impossible things.
326  *What's to do* : what is to be done?
327  *whole* : healthy.

**Brutus**
A piece of work that will make sick men whole.

**Ligarius**
But are not some whole that we must make sick?

**Brutus**
That must we also. What it is, my Caius,
330 I shall unfold to thee as we are going
To whom it must be done.

330  *unfold* : disclose.

**Ligarius**                         Set on your foot,
And with a heart new-fir'd I follow you,

331  *Set . . . foot* : start.
332  *new-fir'd* : with renewed energy.

333    *it sufficeth :* it is enough.

To do I know not what; but it sufficeth
That Brutus leads me on.

**Brutus**                                    Follow me then
                                    [*Exeunt. Thunder*

**Act 2    Scene 2**

Caesar also has been disturbed by the
storm, and he orders the priests to
make a sacrifice to the gods. His wife,
Calphurnia, is very frightened and tries
to persuade Caesar not to go out that
day. Caesar refuses to show fear, but
when the soothsayers warn him of
danger he tells Decius Brutus that he
has decided to stay at home. Decius
replies that Caesar will be laughed at,
and Caesar changes his mind again.
When the conspirators arrive to escort
him to the Capitol, he prepares to go
with them.

sd    *night-gown :* dressing-gown.
3    *Who's within.* Caesar calls for a
servant.
5    *present :* at once.
6    *success :* the result of the sacrifice.
The sacrificial beast was cut open, and
the priests inspected its entrails,
believing that the appearance of the
organs, properly interpreted, could
foretell the future.
8    *What mean you :* what do you
think you are doing.
10    *shall forth :* shall go out.
11    *Ne'er . . . back :* only ever saw
my back.
13    *stood on ceremonies :* paid much
attention to omens.
14    *fright :* frighten.
       *one within :* someone in the house.
16    *watch :* night watchman
(policeman).
17    *whelped :* given birth.
18    *yawn'd :* opened.
20    *right form of war :* correct battle
order.
21    *drizzled blood :* blood fell like rain.
22    *hurtled :* clashed.

**Scene 2** *Rome : Caesar's house*

*Thunder and lightning. Enter* Caesar *in
his night-gown*

**Caesar**

Nor heaven nor earth have been at peace tonight:
Thrice hath Calphurnia in her sleep cried out,
'Help, ho! They murder Caesar!' Who's within?

*Enter a* Servant

**Servant**

My lord!

**Caesar**

5    Go bid the priests do present sacrifice,
And bring me their opinions of success.

**Servant**

I will, my lord.                                    [*Exit*

*Enter* Calphurnia

**Calphurnia**

What mean you, Caesar? Think you to walk forth?
You shall not stir out of your house today.

**Caesar**

10    Caesar shall forth: the things that threaten'd me
Ne'er look'd but on my back; when they shall see
The face of Caesar, they are vanished.

**Calphurnia**

Caesar, I never stood on ceremonies,
Yet now they fright me. There is one within,
15    Besides the things that we have heard and seen,
Recounts most horrid sights seen by the watch.
A lioness hath whelped in the streets,
And graves have yawn'd and yielded up their dead
Fierce fiery warriors fought upon the clouds,
20    In ranks and squadrons and right form of war,
Which drizzled blood upon the Capitol;
The noise of battle hurtl'd in the air,
Horses did neigh, and dying men did groan,

| | |
|---|---|
| 25   *beyond all use :* most unnatural. | And ghosts did shriek and squeal about the streets.<br>25 O Caesar, these things are beyond all use,<br>And I do fear them. |

| | |
|---|---|
| | **Caesar**              What can be avoided |
| 27   *purpos'd :* ordained. | Whose end is purpos'd by the mighty gods?<br>Yet Caesar shall go forth; for these predictions<br>Are to the world in general as to Caesar. |
| 29   Relate to the whole world, not<br>just to Caesar. | **Calphurnia** |
| | 30 When beggars die there are no comets seen;<br>The heavens themselves blaze forth the death of<br>      princes. |
| 31   *blaze forth :* proclaim (in burning<br>meteors). | **Caesar** |
| | Cowards die many times before their deaths;<br>The valiant never taste of death but once. |
| 32   *Cowards . . . deaths :* i.e. in<br>imagination. | Of all the wonders that I yet have heard, |
| 33   *never . . . once :* only experience<br>death once. | 35 It seems to me most strange that men should fear;<br>Seeing that death, a necessary end, |
| 36   *necessary :* inevitable. | Will come when it will come. |
| | *Enter* Servant |
| 37   *augurers :* soothsayers. | What say the augurers? |
| | **Servant** |
| | They would not have you to stir forth today. |
| 39   *offering :* animal sacrificed to the<br>gods. | Plucking the entrails of an offering forth, |

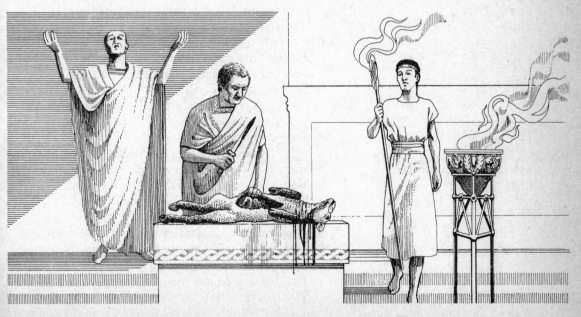

41     *in . . . cowardice :* to make cowards ashamed.

44     *Danger.* Caesar sees danger as a person.

46     *litter'd :* born.

49     *consum'd in :* eaten up by. *confidence :* over-confidence.

56     *for thy humour :* to satisfy your whim.

59     *fetch :* escort.

60     *are :* have. *in very happy time :* at just the right moment.

66     Have I made vast conquests?
67     *afeard :* afraid. *greybeards :* old men.

---

40  They could not find a heart within the beast.
     **Caesar**
  The gods do this in shame of cowardice:
  Caesar should be a beast without a heart
  If he should stay at home today for fear.
  No, Caesar shall not. Danger knows full well
45  That Caesar is more dangerous than he:
  We are two lions litter'd in one day,
  And I the elder and more terrible:
  And Caesar shall go forth.
     **Calphurnia**          Alas! my lord,
  Your wisdom is consum'd in confidence.
50  Do not go forth today: call it my fear
  That keeps you in the house, and not your own.
  We'll send Mark Antony to the Senate House,
  And he shall say you are not well today:
  Let me, upon my knee, prevail in this.
     **Caesar**
55  Mark Antony shall say I am not well;
  And, for thy humour, I will stay at home.

     *Enter* Decius
  Here's Decius Brutus, he shall tell them so.
     **Decius**
  Caesar, all hail! Good morrow, worthy Caesar:
  I come to fetch you to the Senate House.
     **Caesar**
60  And you are come in very happy time
  To bear my greeting to the senators,
  And tell them that I will not come today:
  Cannot, is false, and that I dare not, falser;
  I will not come today: tell them so, Decius.
     **Calphurnia**
65  Say he is sick.
     **Caesar**          Shall Caesar send a lie?
  Have I in conquest stretch'd mine arm so far
  To be afeard to tell greybeards the truth?
  Decius, go tell them Caesar will not come.
     **Decius**
  Most mighty Caesar, let me know some cause,
70  Lest I be laugh'd at when I tell them so.
     **Caesar**
  The cause is in my will: I will not come;
  That is enough to satisfy the senate:

73   *private* : personal.

76   *statue.* For the sake of the rhythm, this word has to be pronounced as three syllables (sta-tu-ay).

78   *lusty* : vigorous.

80   *apply for* : interpret as.

83   *all amiss* : quite wrongly.
84   *fortunate* : promising good fortune.

88-9   *great . . . cognizance* : noble Romans shall crowd around to get something stained by this blood which will serve as a heraldic addition to a coat of arms ('tincture'); an object of reverence ('relic'); and a badge of service ('cognizance'). In Decius's interpretation, the blood is only metaphorical, standing for Caesar's spirit or influence.

91   *expounded* : explained.
92   You will be sure that my explanation is correct when you have heard what else I have to say.

93   *Know it now* : let me tell you now.
      *concluded* : finally decided.

96   *mock* : joke.
97   *Apt* : likely.
      *render'd* : made.

But for your private satisfaction,
Because I love you, I will let you know:
75   Calphurnia here, my wife, stays me at home:
She dreamt tonight she saw my statue,
Which, like a fountain with an hundred spouts,
Did run pure blood; and many lusty Romans
Came smiling, and did bathe their hands in it:
80   And these does she apply for warnings and portents,
And evils imminent; and on her knee
Hath begg'd that I will stay at home today.
   **Decius**
This dream is all amiss interpreted;
It was a vision fair and fortunate:
85   Your statue spouting blood in many pipes,
In which so many smiling Romans bath'd,
Signifies that from you great Rome shall suck
Reviving blood, and that great men shall press
For tinctures, stains, relics, and cognizance.
90   This by Calphurnia's dream is signified.
   **Caesar**
And this way have you well expounded it.
   **Decius**
I have, when you have heard what I can say,
And know it now: the senate have concluded
To give this day a crown to mighty Caesar.
95   If you shall send them word you will not come,
Their minds may change. Besides, it were a mock
Apt to be render'd, for some one to say
'Break up the senate till another time,
When Caesar's wife shall meet with better dreams'.

104    And reason takes second place to love.

100 If Caesar hide himself, shall they not whisper
'Lo! Caesar is afraid'?
Pardon me, Caesar; for my dear dear love
To your proceeding bids me tell you this,
And reason to my love is liable.
**Caesar**
105 How foolish do your fears seem now, Calphurnia!
I am ashamed I did yield to them.
Give me my robe, for I will go:

*Enter* Publius, Brutus, Ligarius, Metellus,
Casca, Trebonius, *and* Cinna
And look where Publius is come to fetch me.
**Publius**
Good morrow, Caesar.
**Caesar**                    Welcome, Publius.
110 What, Brutus, are you stirr'd so early too?
Good morrow, Casca. Caius Ligarius,
Caesar was ne'er so much your enemy
As that same ague which hath made you lean.
What is't o'clock?
**Brutus**            Caesar, 'tis strucken eight.
**Caesar**

*113    ague :* sickness.

*115    pains :* trouble.

115 I thank you for your pains and courtesy.

*Enter* Antony

*116    long o'nights :* late into the night.

See! Antony, that revels long o' nights,
Is notwithstanding up. Good morrow, Antony.
**Antony**
So to most noble Caesar.
**Caesar**                Bid them prepare within:
I am to blame to be thus waited for.
120 Now, Cinna; now, Metellus; what, Trebonius!

*121    in store :* saved up.

I have an hour's talk in store for you;
Remember that you call on me today:
Be near me, that I may remember you.
**Trebonius**
Caesar, I will: [*Aside*] and so near will I be,
125 That your best friends shall wish I had been further.
**Caesar**
Good friends, go in, and taste some wine with me;
And we, like friends, will straightway go together.
**Brutus**

128-9    Brutus's heart grieves ('earns') when he thinks that being *like* a friend is not the same as really *being* a friend.

[*Aside*] That every like is not the same, O Caesar,
The heart of Brutus earns to think upon. [*Exeunt*

## Act 2   Scene 3

Artemidorus reads a letter that he has
written to warn Caesar of the conspiracy
against his life. The episode is narrated
by Plutarch. (See p. 96.)

2     *have an eye to :* keep an eye on.
5     *There . . . men :* these men all
have the same intention.
6     *bent :* directed.
      *beest :* be.
7     *look about you :* be careful what
you do.
      *security :* over-confidence.
      *gives way :* makes room for.
8     *Thy lover :* one who loves you.
10    *suitor :* one who makes a request
(suit).
11–12 *virtue . . . emulation :* virtue cannot exist without being threatened
by other men's jealous rivalry.
14    *the Fates :* the three goddesses
who, in classical mythology, controlled
man's destiny.
      *contrive :* conspire.

## Act 2   Scene 4

Portia is anxious to know what is
happening at the Capitol, and she sends
Lucius to find out. She is so agitated
that she forgets to tell the boy why he
is to go to the Capitol. The Soothsayer
passes by, and says he fears that
something will harm Caesar. This
information alarms Portia still further.

1     *I prithee :* I pray you.
4–5   You would have time to go there
and back before ('Ere') I could think
what it is I want you to do there.
6     *constancy :* strength of purpose.
7     Separate my heart from my
mouth (so that she cannot speak of
what is worrying her).
9     *counsel :* secrets.
10    *yet :* still.

## Scene 3   *Rome : A Street near the Capitol*

*Enter* Artemidorus, *reading a paper*
  **Artemidorus**
*Caesar, beware of Brutus; take heed of Cassius;*
*come not near Casca; have an eye to Cinna; trust not*
*Trebonius; mark well Metellus Cimber; Decius*
*Brutus loves thee not; thou hast wronged Caius*
5 *Ligarius. There is but one mind in all these men, and*
*it is bent against Caesar. If thou beest not immortal,*
*look about you : security gives way to conspiracy.*
*The mighty gods defend thee ! Thy lover,*
                              *Artemidorus.*

Here will I stand till Caesar pass along,
10 And as a suitor will I give him this.
My heart laments that virtue cannot live
Out of the teeth of emulation.
If thou read this, O Caesar, thou may'st live;
If not, the Fates with traitors do contrive.    [*Exit*

## Scene 4   *Rome : outside Brutus's house*

*Enter* Portia *and* Lucius
  **Portia**
I prithee, boy, run to the Senate House;
Stay not to answer me, but get thee gone.
Why dost thou stay?
  **Lucius**                To know my errand, madam.
  **Portia**
I would have had thee there, and here again,
5 Ere I can tell thee what thou shouldst do there.
O constancy, be strong upon my side;
Set a huge mountain 'tween my heart and tongue!
I have a man's mind, but a woman's might.
How hard it is for women to keep counsel!
10 Art thou here yet?
  **Lucius**                Madam, what should I do?
Run to the Capitol, and nothing else?
And so return to you, and nothing else?
  **Portia**
Yes, bring me word, boy, if thy lord look well,

14    *went sickly forth :* was sick when he went out.
         *take good note :* watch carefully.
15    *press :* crowd in on.

18    *bustling rumour :* noise of people rushing about.
         *fray :* fight.

20    *Sooth :* truly.

23    *What is 't o'clock :* what time is it?

25    *stand :* position.

27    *suit :* petition.

29    To do himself a favour and listen to me.

31    *harm's :* harm that is.

32    No harm that I know (for certain) will be, but a great deal of harm that I fear may happen.

35    *praetors :* magistrates.

37    *void :* empty.


For he went sickly forth; and take good note
15  What Caesar doth, what suitors press to him.
Hark, boy! what noise is that?
         **Lucius**
I hear none, madam.
         **Portia**                              Prithee, listen well:
I heard a bustling rumour, like a fray,
And the wind brings it from the Capitol.
         **Lucius**
20  Sooth, madam, I hear nothing.

         *Enter the* Soothsayer
         **Portia**
Come hither, fellow: which way hast thou been?
         **Soothsayer**
At mine own house, good lady.
         **Portia**
What is 't o'clock?
         **Soothsayer**           About the ninth hour, lady.
         **Portia**
Is Caesar yet gone to the Capitol?
         **Soothsayer**
25  Madam, not yet: I go to take my stand,
To see him pass on to the Capitol.
         **Portia**
Thou hast some suit to Caesar, hast thou not?
         **Soothsayer**
That I have, lady: if it will please Caesar
To be so good to Caesar as to hear me,
30  I shall beseech him to befriend himself.
         **Portia**
Why, know'st thou any harm's intended towards him?
         **Soothsayer**
None that I know will be, much that I fear may chance.
Good morrow to you. Here the street is narrow:
The throng that follows Caesar at the heels,
35  Of senators, of praetors, common suitors,
Will crowd a feeble man almost to death:
I'll get me to a place more void, and there
Speak to great Caesar as he comes along.    [*Exit*

**Portia**

I must go in. Ay me, how weak a thing
40  The heart of woman is! O Brutus,
The heavens speed thee in thine enterprise.
[*Aside*] Sure, the boy heard me: Brutus hath a suit
That Caesar will not grant. [*Aside*] O, I grow faint.
Run, Lucius, and commend me to my lord;
45  Say I am merry: come to me again,
And bring me word what he doth say to thee.

[*Exeunt, in different directions*

41       *speed :* favour.
42–3    *Brutus . . . grant.* Portia invents
         an explanation for her anxiety in case
         Lucius did overhear her.
44       *commend me :* give my love.
45       *merry :* cheerful.

# Act 3

Caesar refuses to read the Soothsayer's warning, and the conspirators watch him take his seat in the Senate House. Metellus Cimber kneels before Caesar and presents a petition, which Caesar also refuses to hear. Cimber appeals for help, and this is the signal for the conspirators to stab Caesar, who falls and dies. Brutus takes charge of the situation. Trebonius reports that Mark Antony has fled, but Antony's servant comes with a message of peace. He is followed by Antony himself, who laments briefly over Caesar's body and then expresses his own readiness to be killed by the conspirators. Brutus assures him that he is safe. Antony shakes the hands of the conspirators, and speaks of his love for Caesar. Brutus agrees that Antony shall deliver a funeral oration for Caesar, although Cassius warns Brutus that this is unwise. Alone on the stage at the end of the scene, Antony prophesies civil war, and then sends a message to Octavius Caesar, advising him not to approach Rome just yet. See p. 96.

3      *schedule*: document.
4      *o'er-read*: read through.
5      *your best leisure*: when it is most convenient for you.
7      *touches Caesar nearer*: more closely concerns yourself.
8      *serv'd*: dealt with.
10     *Sirrah*: fellow.
       *place*: way.

**Scene 1**  *Rome: in front of the Capitol*

*A crowd of People, among them* Artemidorus *and the* Soothsayer. *Flourish of trumpets. Enter* Caesar, Brutus, Cassius, Casca, Decius, Metellus, Trebonius, Cinna, Antony, Lepidus, Popilius, Publius, *and Others*

**Caesar**
[*To the* Soothsayer] The ides of March are come.
**Soothsayer**
Ay, Caesar; but not gone.
**Artemidorus**
Hail, Caesar! Read this schedule.
**Decius**
Trebonius doth desire you to o'er-read,
5   At your best leisure, this his humble suit.
**Artemidorus**
O Caesar, read mine first; for mine's a suit
That touches Caesar nearer. Read it, great Caesar.
**Caesar**
What touches us ourself shall be last serv'd.
**Artemidorus**
Delay not, Caesar; read it instantly.
**Caesar**
10  What! is the fellow mad?
**Publius**                          Sirrah, give place.
**Caesar**
What! urge you your petitions in the street?
Come to the Capitol.

        *Caesar goes up to the Senate House, the rest following*

**Popilius**
I wish your enterprise today may thrive.
**Cassius**
What enterprise, Popilius?

**Popilius**                                    Fare you well.
                                        [*Advances to* Caesar

**Brutus**

15 What said Popilius Lena?

**Cassius**

He wish'd today our enterprise might thrive.
I fear our purpose is discovered.

**Brutus**

Look how he makes to Caesar: mark him.

**Cassius**

Casca, be sudden, for we fear prevention.

20 Brutus, what shall be done? If this be known,
Cassius or Caesar never shall turn back,
For I will slay myself.

**Brutus**                    Cassius, be constant.
Popilius Lena speaks not of our purposes;
For, look, he smiles, and Caesar doth not change.

**Cassius**

25 Trebonius knows his time; for, look you, Brutus,
He draws Mark Antony out of the way.
                        [*Exeunt* Antony *and* Trebonius

**Decius**

Where is Metellus Cimber? Let him go,
And presently prefer his suit to Caesar.

**Brutus**

He is address'd; press near and second him.

**Cinna**

30 Casca, you are the first that rears your hand.

**Caesar**

Are we all ready? What is now amiss,
That Caesar and his senate must redress?

**Metellus**

Most high, most mighty, and most puissant Caesar,
Metellus Cimber throws before thy seat
35 A humble heart,—                    [*He kneels*

**Caesar**            I must prevent thee, Cimber.
These couchings and these lowly courtesies
Might fire the blood of ordinary men,
And turn pre-ordinance and first decree
Into the law of children. Be not fond
40 To think that Caesar bears such rebel blood
That will be thaw'd from the true quality
With that which melteth fools—I mean sweet words,

---

18    *makes :* makes his way.

19    *sudden :* quick.
      *we fear prevention :* we are afraid
we shall be stopped.
21    *Cassius or Caesar :* either Cassius
or Caesar.
      *turn back :* return alive.
23    *constant :* steady.

25    *knows his time :* knows when to
      act.

28    *presently :* immediately.
      *prefer :* present.
29    *address'd :* ready.
      *press near :* crowd around.
      *second :* support.
30    *rears :* raises.
31    *amiss :* wrong.
32    *redress :* correct.
33    *puissant :* powerful.
35    *prevent :* forestall.
36    This bowing and this bending
low.
37    *blood :* pride.
38-9  *And . . . children :* and change
order ('ordinance') and law ('decree')
which have been from the beginning
('pre' and 'first') into the rules of a
children's game.
39-42 *Be . . . fools :* do not be foolish
('fond') and think that Caesar's spirit
('blood') can be false ('rebel') to its
real nature ('true quality') and so be
coaxed ('thaw'd') by that which
persuades ('melteth') fools.

43      *Low-crooked curtsies :* knees bending low.
        *base spaniel fawning :* servile cringing like a dog.
44      *decree :* law.
46      *spurn :* kick.
47      *doth not wrong :* does not act unjustly.
47-8    *nor . . . satisfied :* not without good reason ('cause') will he be convinced ('satisfied')—i.e. that the sentence should be repealed.

54      *freedom of repeal :* permission to be recalled from exile.
57      *enfranchisement :* the right to return as a free citizen.
58      *well :* easily.
        *mov'd :* persuaded.
        *as :* like.
59      If I could pray that others would change their minds, then I could myself be persuaded by prayers.
60      *the northern star :* the pole star, which sailors use for steering their course.
61      *resting :* permanent.
62      *no fellow :* nothing like it.
        *firmament :* heavens.
63      *unnumber'd :* innumerable.
65      *but one :* only one.
        *hold his place :* keeps still in the same position.
66      *furnish'd :* stocked.
67      *apprehensive :* rational.
69      *unassailable.* Caesar means that he is not to be persuaded, but another meaning of the word—'cannot be attacked'—lends irony to his speech.
        *holds on his rank :* keeps still in the same position (compare line 65).
70      *Unshak'd of motion :* undisturbed by the movement of objects outside himself.
74      *Olympus :* a mountain in Greece, said to be the home of the gods.
75      *bootless :* without success (the implication is that no-one can succeed where Brutus fails).

Low-crooked curtsies, and base spaniel fawning.
Thy brother by decree is banished :
45 If thou dost bend and pray and fawn for him,
I spurn thee like a cur out of my way.
Know, Caesar doth not wrong, nor without cause
Will he be satisfied.
        **Metellus**
Is there no voice more worthy than my own,
50 To sound more sweetly in great Caesar's ear
For the repealing of my banish'd brother?
        **Brutus**
I kiss thy hand, but not in flattery, Caesar ;
Desiring thee, that Publius Cimber may
Have an immediate freedom of repeal.
        **Caesar**
55 What, Brutus !
        **Cassius**        Pardon, Caesar ; Caesar, pardon :
As low as to thy foot doth Cassius fall,
To beg enfranchisement for Publius Cimber.
        **Caesar**
I could be well mov'd, if I were as you ;
If I could pray to move, prayers would move me ;
60 But I am constant as the northern star,
Of whose true-fix'd and resting quality
There is no fellow in the firmament.
The skies are painted with unnumber'd sparks,
They are all fire and every one doth shine ;
65 But there's but one in all doth hold his place.
So, in the world ; 'tis furnish'd well with men,
And men are flesh and blood, and apprehensive ;
Yet in the number I do know but one
That unassailable holds on his rank,
70 Unshak'd of motion : and that I am he,
Let me a little show it, even in this,
That I was constant Cimber should be banish'd,
And constant do remain to keep him so.
        **Cinna**
O Caesar—
        **Caesar**        Hence ! Wilt thou lift up Olympus !
        **Decius**
75 Great Caesar—
        **Caesar**        Doth not Brutus bootless kneel?

**Casca**

Speak, hands, for me!     [*They stab Caesar*

**Caesar**

*Et tu, Brute?* Then fall, Caesar!     [*Dies*

**Cinna**

Liberty! Freedom! Tyranny is dead!
Run hence, proclaim, cry it about the streets.

**Cassius**

80 Some to the common pulpits, and cry out,
'Liberty, freedom, and enfranchisement!'

**Brutus**

People and senators, be not affrighted;
Fly not; stand still; ambition's debt is paid.

**Casca**

Go to the pulpit, Brutus.

**Decius**                         And Cassius too.

**Brutus**

85 Where's Publius?

**Cinna**

Here, quite confounded with this mutiny.

**Metellus**

Stand fast together, lest some friend of Caesar's
Should chance—

**Brutus**

Talk not of standing. Publius, good cheer;
90 There is no harm intended to your person,
Nor to no Roman else; so tell them, Publius.

**Cassius**

And leave us, Publius; lest that the people,
Rushing on us, should do your age some mischief.

**Brutus**

Do so; and let no man abide this deed
95 But we the doers.

*Enter* Trebonius

**Cassius**

Where's Antony?

**Trebonius**                 Fled to his house amaz'd.
Men, wives and children stare, cry out and run
As it were doomsday.

**Brutus**     Fates, we will know your pleasures.
That we shall die, we know; 'tis but the time
100 And drawing days out, that men stand upon.

77     *Et tu Brute*: even you, Brutus
(*Brute*, in the Latin vocative case, has
two syllables).

80     *common pulpits*: public platforms
for orators.
81     *enfranchisement*: the right to vote.
82     *affrighted*: afraid.
83     *ambition's . . . paid*: we have
given ambition what it deserved.

85     *Publius*: an aged senator, too
weak to run away.

87     *fast*: close.
88     *chance*: happen.

89     *Talk . . . standing*: there's no
need to think of defending ourselves.
*good cheer*: don't worry.

93     *do . . . mischief*: harm you because
you are old.
94     *abide*: face the consequences.

97     *wives*: women.
98     *As it*: as if it.
*doomsday*: the Day of Judgement.
*Fates*: the three goddesses of
destiny.
*your pleasures*: what you have
planned for us.
99-100  We know that we shall die
sometime, and men only worry about
when they will die and how long they
can live.

**Casca**
Why, he that cuts off twenty years of life
Cuts off so many years of fearing death.
**Brutus**

103 *Grant that :* if you agree to that.
104 *abridg'd :* shortened.

Grant that, and then is death a benefit :
So are we Caesar's friends, that have abridg'd
105 His time of fearing death. Stoop, Romans, stoop,
And let us bathe our hands in Caesar's blood
Up to the elbows, and besmear our swords :
Then walk we forth, even to the market-place,
And waving our red weapons o'er our heads,
110 Let's all cry, 'Peace, freedom, and liberty!'
**Cassius**
Stoop, then, and wash. How many ages hence

112 *lofty scene :* noble action.
113 *unborn :* not yet founded.
 *accents :* languages.
114 *in sport :* for entertainment.
115 *Pompey's basis :* the pedestal of
 Pompey's statue.
 *along :* stretched out.
116 *oft :* often.
117 *knot :* band.

Shall this our lofty scene be acted o'er,
In states unborn and accents yet unknown!
**Brutus**
How many times shall Caesar bleed in sport,
115 That now on Pompey's basis lies along
No worthier than the dust!
**Cassius**                    So oft as that shall be,
So often shall the knot of us be call'd
The men that gave their country liberty.
**Decius**

119 *shall we forth :* shall we go out?

What, shall we forth?
**Cassius**                    Ay, every man away :

120 *grace his heels :* honour him by
 following on his heels.

120 Brutus shall lead ; and we will grace his heels
With the most boldest and best hearts of Rome.

*Enter a* Servant
**Brutus**

122 *Soft :* wait.

Soft! who comes here? A friend of Antony's.
**Servant**
Thus, Brutus, did my master bid me kneel ;
Thus did Mark Antony bid me fall down ;
125 And, being prostrate, thus he bade me say :
Brutus is noble, wise, valiant, and honest ;

126 *honest :* honourable.

Caesar was mighty, bold, royal, and loving :
Say I love Brutus, and I honour him ;
Say I fear'd Caesar, honour'd him, and lov'd him.
130 If Brutus will vouchsafe that Antony

130 *vouchsafe :* allow.
131 *resolv'd :* satisfied.

May safely come to him, and be resolv'd
How Caesar hath deserv'd to lie in death,

Mark Antony shall not love Caesar dead
So well as Brutus living; but will follow
135 The fortunes and affairs of noble Brutus
Thorough the hazards of this untrod state
With all true faith. So says my master Antony.

**Brutus**

Thy master is a wise and valiant Roman;
I never thought him worse.
140 Tell him, so please him come unto this place,
He shall be satisfied; and, by my honour,
Depart untouch'd.

**Servant**                                  I'll fetch him presently.
[*Exit*

**Brutus**

I know that we shall have him well to friend.

**Cassius**

I wish we may: but yet have I a mind
145 That fears him much; and my misgiving still
Falls shrewdly to the purpose.

*Enter* Antony

**Brutus**

But here comes Antony. Welcome, Mark Antony.

**Antony**

O mighty Caesar! dost thou lie so low?
Are all thy conquests, glories, triumphs, spoils,
150 Shrunk to this little measure? Fare thee well.
I know not, gentlemen, what you intend,
Who else must be let blood, who else is rank:
If I myself, there is no hour so fit
As Caesar's death's hour, nor no instrument
155 Of half that worth as those your swords, made rich
With the most noble blood of all this world.
I do beseech ye, if ye bear me hard,
Now, whilst your purpled hands do reek and smoke,
Fulfil your pleasure. Live a thousand years,
160 I shall not find myself so apt to die:
No place will please me so, no mean of death,
As here by Caesar, and by you cut off,
The choice and master spirits of this age.

**Brutus**

O Antony, beg not your death of us.
165 Though now we must appear bloody and cruel,
As, by our hands and this our present act,

---

136    *Thorough :* through.
*untrod :* unaccustomed.
*state :* state of affairs.

140    *so please him :* if he will.

142    *presently :* at once.

143    *well to friend :* as a good friend.

145-6    *my . . . purpose :* my suspicions usually ('still') prove to be uncomfortably correct ('to the purpose').

149    *spoils :* trophies.
150    *this little measure :* i.e. the ground his body lies on.
152    *let blood :* killed; a surgeon would draw ('let') blood from a patient for his health.
*rank.* This word combines three meanings: of the same degree as Caesar; overgrown (and so too powerful); corrupted by disease.
155    *Of . . . as :* half as worthy as.
157    *bear me hard :* have any grudge against me.
158    *purpled :* crimson with blood.
*reek :* steam.
159    *Fulfil :* carry out.
*Live :* if I live.
160    *apt :* ready.
161    *mean :* means.
163    *choice :* best.
*master :* most powerful.
164    *beg . . . us :* do not ask us to kill you.

You see we do, yet see you but our hands
And this the bleeding business they have done:
Our hearts you see not; they are pitiful;
170 And pity to the general wrong of Rome—
As fire drives out fire, so pity pity—
Hath done this deed on Caesar. For your part,
To you our swords have leaden points, Mark
    Antony;
Our arms in strength of malice, and our hearts
175 Of brothers' temper, do receive you in
With all kind love, good thoughts, and reverence.
    **Cassius**
Your voice shall be as strong as any man's
In the disposing of new dignities.
    **Brutus**
Only be patient till we have appeas'd
180 The multitude, beside themselves with fear,
And then we will deliver you the cause
Why I, that did love Caesar when I struck him,
Have thus proceeded.
    **Antony**          I doubt not of your wisdom.
Let each man render me his bloody hand:
185 First, Marcus Brutus, will I shake with you;
Next, Caius Cassius, do I take your hand;
Now, Decius Brutus, yours; now yours, Metellus;
Yours, Cinna; and, my valiant Casca, yours;
Though last, not least in love, yours, good
    Trebonius.
190 Gentlemen all—alas! what shall I say?
My credit now stands on such slippery ground,
That one of two bad ways you must conceit me,
Either a coward or a flatterer.
That I did love thee, Caesar, O 'tis true:
195 If then thy spirit look upon us now,
Shall it not grieve thee dearer than thy death,
To see thy Antony making his peace,
Shaking the bloody fingers of thy foes,
Most noble, in the presence of thy corse?
200 Had I as many eyes as thou hast wounds,
Weeping as fast as they stream forth thy blood,
It would become me better than to close
In terms of friendship with thine enemies.

169   *pitiful*: full of pity.
170-2  Just as one fire puts out another, so pity for the injustice suffered by the whole of Rome ('general wrong') meant that we could have no pity on Caesar and drove us to do this deed.
172   *For your part*: as far as you are concerned.
173   *leaden points*: i.e. are harmless.
174-5  Our arms, which appear to be hostile, and our hearts, with the affection of brothers, both welcome you as one of us.
176   *reverence*: respect.
177-8  Your opinion will be taken into consideration as much as anyone else's in the distribution of new offices and honours ('dignities').
181   *deliver . . . cause*: explain the reason to you.
183   *proceeded*: acted.

191   *credit*: reputation.
192   *conceit*: consider.

196   *dearer*: more keenly.

199   *corse*: corpse.

202   *close*: come to an agreement.

204   bay'd . . . hart. A stag ('hart')
is brought to bay when it has been
hunted to a standstill and forced to
face the hounds. The pun with 'heart'
is made clear at line 208. The image is
borrowed from Plutarch—see p. 96.
206   Sign'd: marked.
        spoil: blood; in stag-hunting, the
'spoil' refers to the division of the
animal's body amongst the hounds.
        lethe: life-blood; Lethe was the
river of death in the classical underworld.
207   The whole world was Caesar's
kingdom.
213   modesty: understatement.

215   compact: agreement.
216   prick'd: marked (by making a
prick, or dot, on the list).
217   on: continue.
218   Therefore: for that reason (i.e. to
indicate that I am one of you).
219   Sway'd: diverted.

221   Upon this hope: with the hope
that.
222   wherein: in what way.
223   Or else: if we did not give you
our reasons.
224   good regard: serious considera-
tions.

227   am moreover: as well as this
I would like to ask.
228   Produce: bring out.
230   order: ceremony.

236   will: will go.

Pardon me, Julius! Here wast thou bay'd, brave hart;
205 Here didst thou fall; and here thy hunters stand,
Sign'd in thy spoil, and crimson'd in thy lethe.
O world, thou wast the forest to this hart;
And this indeed, O world, the heart of thee.
How like a deer, strucken by many princes,
210 Dost thou here lie!
        **Cassius**
Mark Antony—
        **Antony**            Pardon me, Caius Cassius:
The enemies of Caesar shall say this;
Then, in a friend, it is cold modesty.
        **Cassius**
I blame you not for praising Caesar so;
215 But what compact mean you to have with us?
Will you be prick'd in number of our friends,
Or shall we on, and not depend on you?
        **Antony**
Therefore I took your hands, but was indeed
Sway'd from the point by looking down on Caesar.
220 Friends am I with you all, and love you all,
Upon this hope, that you shall give me reasons
Why and wherein Caesar was dangerous.
        **Brutus**
Or else were this a savage spectacle.
Our reasons are so full of good regard
225 That were you, Antony, the son of Caesar,
You should be satisfied.
        **Antony**                  That's all I seek;
And am moreover suitor that I may
Produce his body to the market-place,
And in the pulpit, as becomes a friend,
230 Speak in the order of his funeral.
        **Brutus**
You shall, Mark Antony.
        **Cassius**            Brutus, a word with you.
[Aside to Brutus] You know not what you do; do not consent
That Antony speak in his funeral:
Know you how much the people may be mov'd
235 By that which he will utter?
        **Brutus**                  By your pardon;
I will myself into the pulpit first,
And show the reason of our Caesar's death.

238    *protest :* announce.

242    *advantage :* be for our good.

243    *fall :* happen.

246    *devise of :* think of about.

257    *tide of times :* stream of history.
258    *costly :* precious.
260    *ope :* open.
262    *light :* fall.
263    *Domestic :* within the State.
264    *cumber :* burden.
265    *in use :* usual.
267    *but smile :* only smile.
268    *quarter'd :* cut to pieces.
269    *chok'd :* smothered.
       *custom :* familiarity.
       *fell :* terrible.
270    *ranging :* hunting.
271    *Ate :* the Greek personification
    of revenge as a blind goddess of
    discord; there are two syllables in the
    name.
272    *confines :* regions.
273    *Cry 'Havoc'.* Only a king could
    give this order, which was the signal
    for mass slaughter and plunder.

What Antony shall speak, I will protest
He speaks by leave and by permission,
240 And that we are contented Caesar shall
Have all true rites and lawful ceremonies.
It shall advantage more than do us wrong.
   **Cassius**
I know not what may fall; I like it not.
   **Brutus**
Mark Antony, here, take you Caesar's body.
245 You shall not in your funeral speech blame us,
But speak all good you can devise of Caesar,
And say you do 't by our permission;
Else shall you not have any hand at all
About his funeral. And you shall speak
250 In the same pulpit whereto I am going,
After my speech is ended.
   **Antony**           Be it so;
I do desire no more.
   **Brutus**
Prepare the body then, and follow us.
          [*Exeunt all except* Antony
   **Antony**
O, pardon me, thou bleeding piece of earth,
255 That I am meek and gentle with these butchers.
Thou art the ruins of the noblest man
That ever lived in the tide of times.
Woe to the hand that shed this costly blood!
Over thy wounds now do I prophesy,
260 Which like dumb mouths do ope their ruby lips,
To beg the voice and utterance of my tongue:
A curse shall light upon the limbs of men;
Domestic fury and fierce civil strife
Shall cumber all the parts of Italy;
265 Blood and destruction shall be so in use,
And dreadful objects so familiar,
That mothers shall but smile when they behold
Their infants quarter'd with the hands of war,
All pity chok'd with custom of fell deeds;
270 And Caesar's spirit, ranging for revenge,
With Ate by his side come hot from hell,
Shall in these confines with a monarch's voice
Cry 'Havoc!' and let slip the dogs of war,
That this foul deed shall smell above the earth

275    *carrion* : dead.

275    With carrion men, groaning for burial.

*Enter a* Servant

You serve Octavius Caesar, do you not?
**Servant**
I do, Mark Antony.
**Antony**
Caesar did write for him to come to Rome.
**Servant**
He did receive his letters, and is coming;
280    And bid me say to you by word of mouth—
                    [*Seeing the body*

O Caesar!—
**Antony**
Thy heart is big; get thee apart and weep.

282    *big* : swollen with grief.
283    *Passion* : emotion.
284    *beads of sorrow* : tears.

Passion, I see, is catching; for mine eyes,
Seeing those beads of sorrow stand in thine,
285    Began to water. Is thy master coming?
**Servant**
He lies tonight within seven leagues of Rome.

286    *lies* : is in camp.
       *seven leagues* : about twenty-one
miles.
287    *Post* : ride fast.
       *chanc'd* : happened.

**Antony**
Post back with speed, and tell him what hath
    chanc'd.
Here is a mourning Rome, a dangerous Rome,
No Rome of safety for Octavius yet;

290    *Hie* : hurry.
291    *not back* : not go back.
292    *try* : test.
293    *take* : react to.
294    *cruel issue* : results of the cruelty.
295    *According . . . which* : depending
on which (i.e. the citizens' reactions).
       *discourse* : describe.

290    Hie hence and tell him so. Yet, stay awhile;
Thou shalt not back till I have borne this corpse
Into the market-place; there shall I try,
In my oration, how the people take
The cruel issue of these bloody men;
295    According to the which thou shalt discourse
To young Octavius of the state of things.
Lend me your hand.
                    [*Exeunt, with* Caesar's *body*

**Act 3    Scene 2**
The citizens demand to know why
Caesar was murdered, and Brutus
addresses them. He tells them that he
loved Caesar, but that he loved
freedom even more. This answer
satisfies the people, and they are ready
to accept Brutus in Caesar's place.

**Scene 2** *Rome : the Forum*

*Enter* Brutus *and* Cassius, *and a crowd of*
Citizens.
**Citizens**
We will be satisfied: let us be satisfied.

Brutus asks them to listen to Mark Antony's funeral oration, and they are obedient. Antony's powerful speech describes Caesar in loving terms, telling of his love for Rome and his sympathy for the Romans. He displays Caesar's body, and points to the many wounds. The citizens are provoked to the point of mutiny, and after Antony has read Caesar's will they riot, threatening the lives of the conspirators. At the end of the scene Antony is told that Octavius and Lepidus have entered Rome, whilst Brutus and Cassius have fled from the city. The idea for this scene was supplied by Plutarch. (See p. 97.)

1     *satisfied :* given a satisfactory explanation.
2     *give me audience :* listen to me.
4     *part the numbers :* divide the crowd.
7     *public reasons :* reasons concerning the public good.
10    *severally :* separately.
12    *till the last :* until the end.
13    *lovers :* dear friends.
13-14 *for my cause :* for the sake of the cause I represent.
14-16 *believe me . . . may believe :* believe me, because you know that I am a man of honour; and remember that I am honourable, and therefore you may believe me.
16    *Censure :* judge.
17    *senses :* understanding.
23    *Had you :* would you.
26    *fortunate :* successful (in war).

30    *would be :* would wish to be.

32    *rude :* uncivilized.

**Brutus**
Then follow me, and give me audience, friends.
Cassius, go you into the other street,
And part the numbers.
5 Those that will hear me speak, let 'em stay here;
Those that will follow Cassius, go with him;
And public reasons shall be rendered
Of Caesar's death.
    **First Citizen**     I will hear Brutus speak.
    **Second Citizen**
I will hear Cassius; and compare their reasons,
10 When severally we hear them rendered.
        [*Exit* Cassius, *with some of the* Citizens;
        Brutus *goes into the pulpit*
    **Third Citizen**
The noble Brutus is ascended: silence!
    **Brutus**
Be patient till the last.
Romans, countrymen, and lovers! hear me for my cause; and be silent, that you may hear. Believe me
15 for mine honour, and have respect to mine honour, that you may believe. Censure me in your wisdom, and awake your senses, that you may the better judge. If there be any in this assembly, any dear friend of Caesar's, to him I say, that Brutus' love
20 to Caesar was no less than his. If then that friend demand why Brutus rose against Caesar, this is my answer: not that I loved Caesar less, but that I loved Rome more. Had you rather Caesar were living, and die all slaves, than that Caesar were dead, to
25 live all free men? As Caesar loved me, I weep for him; as he was fortunate, I rejoice at it; as he was valiant, I honour him; but, as he was ambitious, I slew him. There is tears for his love; joy for his fortune; honour for his valour; and death for his
30 ambition. Who is here so base that would be a bondman? If any, speak; for him have I offended. Who is here so rude that would not be a Roman? If any, speak; for him have I offended. Who is here so vile that will not love his country? If any, speak;
35 for him have I offended. I pause for a reply.
    **Citizens**
None, Brutus, none.

**Brutus**
Then none have I offended. I have done no more to
Caesar, than you shall do to Brutus. The question
40 of his death is enrolled in the Capitol; his glory not
extenuated, wherein he was worthy; nor his
offences enforced, for which he suffered death.

*Enter* Antony *and Others, with* Caesar's
*body*

Here comes his body, mourned by Mark Antony;
who, though he had no hand in his death, shall
receive the benefit of his dying, a place in the
45 commonwealth; as which of you shall not? With
this I depart: that, as I slew my best lover for the
good of Rome, I have the same dagger for myself,
when it shall please my country to need my death.
    **Citizens**
Live, Brutus! live! live!
    **First Citizen**
50 Bring him with triumph home unto his house.
    **Second Citizen**
Give him a statue with his ancestors.
    **Third Citizen**
Let him be Caesar.
    **Fourth Citizen**                Caesar's better parts
Shall be crown'd in Brutus.
    **First Citizen**
We'll bring him to his house with shouts and
    clamours.
    **Brutus**
55 My countrymen—
    **Second Citizen**  Peace! silence! Brutus speaks.
    **First Citizen**
Peace, ho!
    **Brutus**
Good countrymen, let me depart alone,
And, for my sake, stay here with Antony.
Do grace to Caesar's corpse, and grace his speech
60 Tending to Caesar's glories, which Mark Antony,
By our permission, is allow'd to make.
I do entreat you, not a man depart,
Save I alone, till Antony have spoke.        [*Exit*
    **First Citizen**
Stay, ho! and let us hear Mark Antony.

---

38  *do to Brutus*: i.e. if Brutus becomes a tyrant.
38–9  *question of*: reasons for.
39  *enrolled*: recorded in the archives.
    *glory*: noble deeds.
40  *extenuated*: belittled.
41  *enforced*: emphasized.

43  *no hand in*: was not responsible for.
44–5  *a place in the commonwealth*: the right to live in a free republic.
46  *lover*: friend.

52  *parts*: qualities.

59  *Do grace*: honour.
    *and grace*: and respect.
60  *Tending to*: referring to.

**Third Citizen**

65 Let him go up into the public chair;
We'll hear him. Noble Antony, go up.

**Antony**

For Brutus' sake, I am beholding to you.

                                             *[Goes into the pulpit*

**Fourth Citizen**

What does he say of Brutus?

**Third Citizen**         He says, for Brutus' sake,
He finds himself beholding to us all.

**Fourth Citizen**

70 'Twere best he speak no harm of Brutus here.

**First Citizen**

This Caesar was a tyrant.

**Third Citizen**            Nay, that's certain:
We are bless'd that Rome is rid of him.

**Second Citizen**

Peace! let us hear what Antony can say.

**Antony**

You gentle Romans—

**Citizens**              Peace, ho! let us hear him.

**Antony**

75 Friends, Romans, countrymen, lend me your ears;
I come to bury Caesar, not to praise him.
The evil that men do lives after them,
The good is oft interred with their bones;
So let it be with Caesar. The noble Brutus

80 Hath told you Caesar was ambitious;
If it were so, it was a grievous fault,
And grievously hath Caesar answer'd it.
Here, under leave of Brutus and the rest—
For Brutus is an honourable man;

85 So are they all, all honourable men—
Come I to speak in Caesar's funeral.
He was my friend, faithful and just to me;
But Brutus says he was ambitious,
And Brutus is an honourable man.

90 He hath brought many captives home to Rome,
Whose ransoms did the general coffers fill:
Did this in Caesar seem ambitious?
When that the poor have cried, Caesar hath wept;
Ambition should be made of sterner stuff:

95 Yet Brutus says he was ambitious,
And Brutus is an honourable man.

---

**Glossary (left margin):**

65   *public chair*: orator's platform.

67   *For Brutus' sake*: on behalf of Brutus (whom the people were obeying in listening to Antony).
    *beholding*: indebted.

75   *lend . . . ears*: listen to me.

78   *interred*: buried—i.e. forgotten.

83   *under leave of*: with permission from.

91   *general coffers*: public treasury.

94   *sterner*: stronger.

**97** *on the Lupercal :* on the feast of Lupercal (see note on *1, 1, 70*).

**102** *disprove :* contradict.

**105** *withholds :* prevents.

**110** *Methinks :* I think.

**114** *Mark'd . . . words :* did you hear what he said.

**116** *be found :* can be proved.
*dear abide it :* pay dearly for it.

**119** *mark :* listen to.
**120** *But :* only.
**121** *stood against :* overcome the opposition of.
**122** No man is so humble as to look up to him.
**123** *dispos'd :* inclined.
**128** *wrong the dead :* i.e. by not defending Caesar from being called ambitious.
*wrong myself :* i.e. by not speaking what I know to be true.
*and you :* i.e. by allowing you to be deceived by Brutus.
**130** *parchment :* document.
**131** *closet :* study.

You all did see that on the Lupercal
I thrice presented him a kingly crown,
Which he did thrice refuse : was this ambition?
100 Yet Brutus says he was ambitious,
And, sure, he is an honourable man.
I speak not to disprove what Brutus spoke,
But here I am to speak what I do know.
You all did love him once, not without cause :
105 What cause withholds you then to mourn for him?
O judgment, thou art fled to brutish beasts,
And men have lost their reason. Bear with me;
My heart is in the coffin there with Caesar,
And I must pause till it come back to me.
**First Citizen**
110 Methinks there is much reason in his sayings.
**Second Citizen**
If thou consider rightly of the matter,
Caesar has had great wrong.
**Third Citizen**                Has he, masters?
I fear there will a worse come in his place.
**Fourth Citizen**
Mark'd ye his words? He would not take the crown;
115 Therefore 'tis certain he was not ambitious.
**First Citizen**
If it be found so, some will dear abide it.
**Second Citizen**
Poor soul! his eyes are red as fire with weeping.
**Third Citizen**
There's not a nobler man in Rome than Antony.
**Fourth Citizen**
Now mark him; he begins again to speak.
**Antony**
120 But yesterday the word of Caesar might
Have stood against the world; now lies he there,
And none so poor to do him reverence.
O masters! if I were dispos'd to stir
Your hearts and minds to mutiny and rage,
125 I should do Brutus wrong, and Cassius wrong,
Who, you all know, are honourable men.
I will not do them wrong; I rather choose
To wrong the dead, to wrong myself, and you,
Than I will wrong such honourable men.
130 But here's a parchment with the seal of Caesar;
I found it in his closet, 'tis his will.

132 *commons* : citizens.
    *testament* : will.

135 *napkins* : handkerchiefs.

139 *issue* : children.

143 *meet* : fitting.

152 *o'ershot myself* : gone too far.

Let but the commons hear this testament—
Which, pardon me, I do not mean to read—
And they would go and kiss dead Caesar's wounds
135 And dip their napkins in his sacred blood,
Yea, beg a hair of him for memory,
And, dying, mention it within their wills,
Bequeathing it as a rich legacy
Unto their issue.

**Fourth Citizen**
140 We'll hear the will: read it, Mark Antony.

**Citizens**
The will, the will! we will hear Caesar's will.

**Antony**
Have patience, gentle friends; I must not read it:
It is not meet you know how Caesar lov'd you.
You are not wood, you are not stones, but men;
145 And, being men, hearing the will of Caesar,
It will inflame you, it will make you mad.
'Tis good you know not that you are his heirs;
For if you should, O, what would come of it?

**Fourth Citizen**
Read the will, we'll hear it, Antony!
150 You shall read us the will, Caesar's will.

**Antony**
Will you be patient? Will you stay awhile?
I have o'ershot myself to tell you of it.
I fear I wrong the honourable men
Whose daggers have stabb'd Caesar; I do fear it.

**Fourth Citizen**
155 They were traitors. Honourable men!

**Citizens**
The will! the testament!

**Second Citizen**
They were villains, murderers. The will! read the
will!

**Antony**
You will compel me then to read the will?
Then make a ring about the corpse of Caesar,
160 And let me show you him that made the will.
Shall I descend? and will you give me leave?

**Citizens**
Come down.

**Second Citizen**
Descend.                              [Antony *comes down*
**Third Citizen**
You shall have leave.
**Fourth Citizen**
165 A ring; stand round.
**First Citizen**
Stand from the hearse; stand from the body.
**Second Citizen**
Room for Antony; most noble Antony.
**Antony**
Nay, press not so upon me; stand far off.
**Citizens**
Stand back! room! bear back!
**Antony**
170 If you have tears, prepare to shed them now.
You all do know this mantle: I remember
The first time ever Caesar put it on;
'Twas on a summer's evening, in his tent,
That day he overcame the Nervii.
175 Look, in this place ran Cassius' dagger through:
See what a rent the envious Casca made:
Through this the well-beloved Brutus stabb'd;
And, as he pluck'd his cursed steel away,
Mark how the blood of Caesar follow'd it,
180 As rushing out of doors, to be resolv'd
If Brutus so unkindly knock'd or no;
For Brutus, as you know, was Caesar's angel:
Judge, O you gods, how dearly Caesar lov'd him.
This was the most unkindest cut of all;
185 For when the noble Caesar saw him stab,
Ingratitude, more strong than traitors' arms,
Quite vanquish'd him: then burst his mighty heart;
And, in his mantle muffling up his face,
Even at the base of Pompey's statue,
190 Which all the while ran blood, great Caesar fell.
O, what a fall was there, my countrymen!
Then I, and you, and all of us fell down,
Whilst bloody treason flourish'd over us.
O, now you weep, and I perceive you feel
195 The dint of pity; these are gracious drops.
Kind souls, what, weep you when you but behold
Our Caesar's vesture wounded? Look you here,

168   *far :* further.

171   *mantle :* cloak.

174   *the Nervii :* the most warlike of
the Gallic tribes, whom Caesar
conquered in 57 B.C.; he himself fought
valiantly in the battle, and his victory
was celebrated with more than usual
rejoicing in Rome.
176   *envious :* malicious.
180   *be resolv'd :* make sure.
181   *unkindly :* both 'cruelly' and
'unnaturally'.
182   *angel :* favourite.

184   *most unkindest cut :* the wound
that hurt most.
186   *Ingratitude :* the blow struck by
Brutus's ingratitude.

190   *Which . . . blood.* Caesar's blood
was pouring out all over the statue, so
that it seemed as though the statue was
bleeding.
193   *flourish'd :* triumphed.
195   *dint :* blow.
       *gracious :* honourable.
196   *but :* only.
197   *vesture :* clothing.

198    *marr'd :* mutilated.

Here is himself, marr'd, as you see, with traitors.

**First Citizen**
O piteous spectacle!

**Second Citizen**
200 O noble Caesar!

**Third Citizen**
O woeful day!

**Fourth Citizen**
O traitors! villains!

**First Citizen**
O most bloody sight!

**Second Citizen**
We will be revenged.

**Citizens**

205    *About :* set about doing it.

205 Revenge!—About!—Seek!—Burn!—Fire!—Kill!
    —Slay! Let not a traitor live.

**Antony**
Stay, countrymen!

**First Citizen**
Peace there! Hear the noble Antony.

**Second Citizen**
We'll hear him, we'll follow him, we'll die with him.

**Antony**
210 Good friends, sweet friends, let me not stir you up

211    *flood of mutiny :* wave of violence.

To such a sudden flood of mutiny.
They that have done this deed are honourable :

213    *private griefs :* personal
grievances.

What private griefs they have, alas, I know not,
That made them do it; they are wise and
    honourable,
215 And will, no doubt, with reasons answer you.
I come not, friends, to steal away your hearts;
I am no orator, as Brutus is,
But, as you know me all, a plain blunt man,
That love my friend; and that they know full well

220    *public . . . speak :* permission to
speak in public.
221    *wit :* intelligence.
    *worth :* authority.
222    *Action :* gesture.
    *utterance :* elocution.
    *power of speech :* rhetoric.
223    *right on :* directly.

220 That gave me public leave to speak of him.
For I have neither wit, nor words, nor worth,
Action, nor utterance, nor the power of speech,
To stir men's blood: I only speak right on;
I tell you that which you yourselves do know,
225 Show you sweet Caesar's wounds, poor poor dumb
    mouths,
And bid them speak for me. But were I Brutus,
And Brutus Antony, there were an Antony

228   *ruffle* : stir.

Would ruffle up your spirits, and put a tongue
In every wound of Caesar, that should move
230 The stones of Rome to rise and mutiny.

**Citizens**
We'll mutiny.

**First Citizen**
We'll burn the house of Brutus.

**Third Citizen**
Away, then! come, seek the conspirators.

**Antony**
Yet hear me, countrymen; yet hear me speak.

**Citizens**
235 Peace, ho!—Hear Antony, most noble Antony.

**Antony**
Why, friends, you go to do you know not what.

237   *Wherein* : in what way?

Wherein hath Caesar thus deserv'd your loves?
Alas! you know not: I must tell you then.
You have forgot the will I told you of.

**Citizens**
240 Most true. The will! let's stay and hear the will.

**Antony**
Here is the will, and under Caesar's seal.
To every Roman citizen he gives,

243   *several* : individual.
    *drachmas* : silver coins.

To every several man, seventy-five drachmas.

**Second Citizen**
Most noble Caesar! we'll revenge his death.

**Third Citizen**

245   *royal* : generous.

245 O royal Caesar!

**Antony**
Hear me with patience.

**Citizens**
Peace, ho!

**Antony**
Moreover, he hath left you all his walks,

248   *walks* : gardens.
249   *His private arbours* : his own
summer-houses.
    *new-planted* : freshly planted.
251   *common pleasures* : public
pleasure-gardens.
252   *abroad* : in the open air.
255   *the holy place* : the Forum, centre
of religious as well as political life in
Rome. See p. 97.
256   *brands* : burning wood from the
funeral pyre.

His private arbours, and new-planted orchards,
250 On this side Tiber; he hath left them you,
And to your heirs for ever; common pleasures,
To walk abroad, and recreate yourselves.
Here was a Caesar! when comes such another?

**First Citizen**
Never, never! Come, away, away!
255 We'll burn his body in the holy place,
And with the brands fire the traitors' houses.

**Second Citizen**
Go fetch fire.

**Third Citizen**
Pluck down benches.

259    *Pluck* : pull.

**Fourth Citizen**
260 Pluck down forms, windows, any thing.
[*Exeunt* Citizens, *with the body*

**Antony**

261    *afoot* : begun.

Now let it work: mischief, thou art afoot,
Take thou what course thou wilt!

*Enter a* Servant
How now, fellow!

**Servant**
Sir, Octavius is already come to Rome.

**Antony**
Where is he?

**Servant**
265 He and Lepidus are at Caesar's house.

**Antony**

267    *upon a wish* : just as I wished.
      *Fortune* : i.e. the goddess Fortune.

And thither will I straight to visit him.
He comes upon a wish. Fortune is merry,
And in this mood will give us any thing.

**Servant**
I heard him say Brutus and Cassius

270    *Are rid* : have ridden.

270 Are rid like madmen through the gates of Rome.

**Antony**

271    *Belike* : probably.
271-2  *some . . . them* : some warning
       about how I have influenced the
       citizens.

Belike they had some notice of the people,
How I had mov'd them. Bring me to Octavius.
[*Exeunt*

**Act 3   Scene 3**
Cinna the poet is wandering through
the streets of Rome when he meets a
crowd of angry citizens. They ask
questions, and when he tells them his
name they kill him, simply because
Cinna is the name of one of the
conspirators. Shakespeare dramatizes
Plutarch—see p. 98.

1      *tonight* : last night.

**Scene 3** *Rome : a street*

*Enter* Cinna *the Poet*

**Cinna**
I dreamt tonight that I did feast with Caesar,

charge : fill.
fantasy : imagination.
will : desire.
forth of doors : outside.

And things unluckily charge my fantasy.
I have no will to wander forth of doors,
Yet something leads me forth.

*Enter* Citizens

**First Citizen**

5 What is your name?

**Second Citizen**

Whither are you going?

**Third Citizen**

Where do you dwell?

**Fourth Citizen**

Are you a married man or a bachelor?

**Second Citizen**

Answer every man directly.

**First Citizen**

10 Ay, and briefly.

**Fourth Citizen**

Ay, and wisely.

**Third Citizen**

you were best : you had better.

Ay, and truly, you were best.

**Cinna**

What is my name? Whither am I going? Where
do I dwell? Am I a married man or a bachelor?

15 Then, to answer every man directly and briefly,
wisely and truly: wisely I say, I am a bachelor.

**Second Citizen**

That's as much as to say, they are fools that marry;

bear me a bang : get a blow from
me.

directly. The citizen intends
'plainly', but Cinna means
'immediately'.

you'll bear me a bang for that, I fear. Proceed;
directly.

**Cinna**

20 Directly, I am going to Caesar's funeral.

**First Citizen**

As a friend or an enemy?

**Cinna**

As a friend.

**Second Citizen**

That matter is answered directly.

**Fourth Citizen**

For your dwelling : where do you
live.

For your dwelling, briefly.

**Cinna**

25 Briefly, I dwell by the Capitol.

**Third Citizen**

Your name, sir, truly.

**Cinna**

Truly, my name is Cinna.

**Second Citizen**

Tear him to pieces! He's a conspirator.

**Cinna**

I am Cinna the poet, I am Cinna the poet.

**Fourth Citizen**

30 Tear him for his bad verses, tear him for his bad
verses.

**Cinna**

I am not Cinna the conspirator.

**Second Citizen**

33    *pluck but :* simply tear.

34    *turn him going :* set him free.

It is no matter, his name's Cinna; pluck but his
name out of his heart, and turn him going.

**Third Citizen**

35 Tear him, tear him! Come, brands, ho! firebrands!
To Brutus', to Cassius'; burn all. Some to Decius'
house, and some to Casca's; some to Ligarius'.
Away! go!                                    [*Exeunt*

# Act 4

**Act 4  Scene 1**
Antony, Octavius and Lepidus are
planning their campaign against the
conspirators. Antony despises Lepidus,
and plans to discard him when he has
served his purpose.

1   *These many* : so many.
    *prick'd* : ticked off (with a pin-
prick on the list).

4   *Upon condition* : on condition
that.

6   *damn* : condemn.

9   How to pay for some of the
expenses from the legacies in Caesar's
will.

11  *Or . . . or* : either . . . or.
12  *slight* : weak.
    *unmeritable* : unworthy.
13  *Meet* : suitable.
    *fit* : right.
14  *The . . . divided* : when the world
is divided into three parts (Europe,
Africa and Asia).
14–15  *he . . . it* : that he should be
considered as one of the three rulers.
16  *voice* : vote.
    *prick'd* : chosen.
17  In our cruel sentence of death
and exile.
18  *I . . . you* : I am older and more
experienced than you.
20  To take away some of the blame
from ourselves.
21  *them* : i.e. the honours.

**Scene 1** *Rome : A Room in Antony's House*

*Enter* Antony, Octavius, *and* Lepidus

**Antony**
These many then shall die ; their names are prick'd.
**Octavius**
Your brother too must die ; consent you, Lepidus ?
**Lepidus**
I do consent—
**Octavius**                    Prick him down, Antony.
**Lepidus**
Upon condition Publius shall not live,
5 Who is your sister's son, Mark Antony.
**Antony**
He shall not live ; look, with a spot I damn him.
But, Lepidus, go you to Caesar's house ;
Fetch the will hither, and we shall determine
How to cut off some charge in legacies.
**Lepidus**
10 What, shall I find you here ?
**Octavius**
Or here or at the Capitol.            [*Exit* Lepidus
**Antony**
This is a slight unmeritable man,
Meet to be sent on errands. Is it fit,
The three-fold world divided, he should stand
15 One of the three to share it ?
**Octavius**                    So you thought him ;
And took his voice who should be prick'd to die,
In our black sentence and proscription.
**Antony**
Octavius, I have seen more days than you ;
And though we lay these honours on this man,
20 To ease ourselves of divers sland'rous loads,
He shall but bear them as the ass bears gold,

24    *will* : wish.
25    *turn him off* : set him loose.
26    *empty* : unburdened.
      *shake his ears* : look like an ass.
27    And pick up what he can find
with all the others.
      *your will* : as you like.
28    *tried* : experienced.
30    *appoint* : allow.
      *store of provender* : supply of food.
32    *wind* : turn.
33    His body is directed by my mind.
34    *in some taste* : to some extent.
      *but so* : no more than that.
36    *barren-spirited* : with no ideas of
his own.
37    *abject* : rejected.
      *orts* : scraps.
38    *use* : fashion.
      *stal'd* : worn out.
39    *Begin his fashion* : seem new to
him.
40    *But as a property* : except as a
tool.
42    *levying powers* : raising armies.
      *straight* : immediately.
      *make head* : advance against them.
43    *let . . . combined* : let our allied
troops be united in one army.
44    Get support from our friends,
and make the most of our resources.
45    *presently* : at once.
      *sit in council* : decide.
46    How things which are not yet
known to the public should be revealed.
47    And how obvious dangers can
best be dealt with.
48-9  We are tied to a post ('stake')
and threatened ('bay'd about') by a
lot of enemies—just as a captured bear
is tied up and tormented by hounds.
51    *mischiefs* : dangerous plans.

**Act 4   Scene 2**

In the rebel camp, Brutus and Cassius
are no longer the close friends that they
used to be.

To groan and sweat under the business,
Either led or driven, as we point the way;
And having brought our treasure where we will,
25 Then take we down his load, and turn him off,
Like to the empty ass, to shake his ears,
And graze in commons.
      **Octavius**              You may do your will;
But he's a tried and valiant soldier.
      **Antony**
So is my horse, Octavius; and for that
30 I do appoint him store of provender.
It is a creature that I teach to fight,
To wind, to stop, to run directly on,
His corporal motion govern'd by my spirit.
And, in some taste, is Lepidus but so;
35 He must be taught, and train'd, and bid go forth:
A barren-spirited fellow; one that feeds
On abject orts, and imitations,
Which, out of use and stal'd by other men,
Begin his fashion. Do not talk of him
40 But as a property. And now, Octavius,
Listen great things. Brutus and Cassius
Are levying powers; we must straight make head.
Therefore let our alliance be combin'd,
Our best friends made, and our means stretch'd;
45 And let us presently go sit in council,
How covert matters may be best disclos'd,
And open perils surest answered.
      **Octavius**
Let us do so: for we are at the stake,
And bay'd about with many enemies;
50 And some that smile have in their hearts, I fear,
Millions of mischiefs.              [*Exeunt*

**Scene 2** *Sardis : the rebel camp*

*Drum. Enter* Brutus, Lucilius, Lucius,
*and* Soldiers : Titinius *and* Pindarus *meet
them*

| | |
|---|---|
| 1 | *Stand :* halt. |
| 2 | *word :* password. |
| 4 | *at hand :* near by. |
| 5 | *do you salutation :* bring you greetings. |
| 7 | *In . . . change :* because of some change in himself. |
| | *by ill officers :* because of the bad conduct of his officers. |
| 8 | *worthy cause :* good reason. |
| 10 | *be satisfied :* be given an explanation. |
| 12 | *full of regard :* entirely deserving of respect. |
| 14 | *let . . . resolv'd :* tell me. |
| 16 | *familiar instances :* evidence of close friendship. |
| 17 | *free . . . conference :* open and friendly conversation. |
| 18 | *As . . . old :* that he has shown in the past. |
| 19 | *Ever :* always. |
| 21 | *enforced :* constrained, unnatural. |
| | *ceremony :* formality. |
| 22 | *tricks :* deceits. |
| | *faith :* friendship. |
| 23 | *hollow :* insincere. |
| | *hot at hand :* eager so long as they are held back. |
| 24 | *mettle :* spirit. |
| 26 | *fall :* droop. |
| | *crests :* proud necks. |
| | *jades :* worthless horses. |
| 27 | *Sink in the trial :* fail when they are put to the test. |
| 29 | *horse in general :* main part of the cavalry. |

**Brutus**
Stand, ho!
**Lucilius**
Give the word, ho! and stand.
**Brutus**
What now, Lucilius! is Cassius near?
**Lucilius**
He is at hand; and Pindarus is come
5 To do you salutation from his master.
[*Pindarus gives a letter to* Brutus
**Brutus**
[*Reading the letter*] He greets me well. Your master, Pindarus,
In his own change, or by ill officers,
Hath given me some worthy cause to wish
Things done, undone; but, if he be at hand,
10 I shall be satisfied.
**Pindarus**                                    I do not doubt
But that my noble master will appear
Such as he is, full of regard and honour.
**Brutus**
He is not doubted. A word, Lucilius;
How he receiv'd you, let me be resolv'd.
**Lucilius**
15 With courtesy and with respect enough,
But not with such familiar instances,
Nor with such free and friendly conference,
As he hath us'd of old.
**Brutus**                                    Thou hast describ'd
A hot friend cooling. Ever note, Lucilius,
20 When love begins to sicken and decay,
It useth an enforced ceremony.
There are no tricks in plain and simple faith;
But hollow men, like horses hot at hand,
Make gallant show and promise of their mettle;
25 But when they should endure the bloody spur,
They fall their crests, and, like deceitful jades,
Sink in the trial. Comes his army on?
**Lucilius**
They mean this night in Sardis to be quarter'd;
The greater part, the horse in general,
30 Are come with Cassius. [*Sound of marching, within*

**Brutus**                                    Hark! he is arriv'd.
March gently on to meet him.

*Enter* Cassius *and* Soldiers

**Cassius**
Stand, ho!

**Brutus**
Stand, ho! Speak the word along.

**First Soldier**
Stand!

**Second Soldier**
35 Stand!

**Third Soldier**
Stand!

**Cassius**
Most noble brother, you have done me wrong.

**Brutus**
Judge me, you gods! Wrong I mine enemies?
And, if not so, how should I wrong a brother?

**Cassius**
40 Brutus, this sober form of yours hides wrongs;
And when you do them—

**Brutus**                                    Cassius, be content;
Speak your griefs softly: I do know you well.
Before the eyes of both our armies here,
Which should perceive nothing but love from us,
45 Let us not wrangle. Bid them move away;
Then in my tent, Cassius, enlarge your griefs,
And I will give you audience.

**Cassius**                                          Pindarus,
Bid our commanders lead their charges off
A little from this ground.

**Brutus**
50 Lucius, do you the like; and let no man
Come to our tent till we have done our conference.
Let Lucilius and Titinius guard our door.   [*Exeunt*

33   *Speak . . . along :* pass the order
(to halt) along the line.

37   *done me wrong :* injured me.

38   *Wrong I :* do I injure?

40   *sober form :* dignified manner.

41   *content :* calm.

42   *griefs :* grievances.
     *softly :* quietly.

46   *enlarge your griefs :* tell me your
grievances in full.

47   *give you audience :* listen to you.

48   *charges :* forces under their
command.

50   *do you the like :* you do the same.

## Act 4  Scene 3

Brutus accuses Cassius of a greed for
gold which has led him to betray their
cause. The two men insult each other
angrily, but eventually become friends
again. A poet comes to the tent and
tries to act as peacemaker, but Brutus
is scornful and sends him away. Then
he explains to Cassius that the real
reason for his short temper is grief,
because he has just heard that Portia,
his wife, is dead. Messala comes to
discuss the letters he has received from
Rome, with the news of Portia's death
(see Introduction p. xxii). Brutus
explains why it is necessary for their
armies to advance on Philippi, where
they will meet Antony and the Roman
forces. Cassius leaves him to go to bed,
and Brutus calls for Varro and
Claudius to sleep in his tent. But
Brutus cannot sleep, and he is visited

## Scene 3  *Sardis : inside the Tent of Brutus*

### *Enter* Brutus *and* Cassius

**Cassius**

That you have wrong'd me doth appear in this:
You have condemn'd and noted Lucius Pella
For taking bribes here of the Sardians;
Wherein my letters, praying on his side,
5 Because I knew the man, were slighted off.

**Brutus**

You wrong'd yourself to write in such a case.

**Cassius**

In such a time as this it is not meet
That every nice offence should bear his comment.

**Brutus**

Let me tell you, Cassius, you yourself
10 Are much condemn'd to have an itching palm,
To sell and mart your offices for gold
To undeservers.

by the ghost of Caesar, which tells him
that they will meet again at Philippi.
Brutus wakes Varro and Claudius, who
have seen nothing. These events are
narrated by Plutarch. (See pp. 98–9.)

1     *wrong'd* : injured.
    *doth appear* : is evident.

2     *condemn'd* : found guilty.
    *noted* : disgraced.

4     *praying . . . side* : pleading on his
behalf.

5     *I knew the man* : he was a friend
of mine.
    *slighted off* : dismissed.

8     *nice* : trivial.
    *his comment* : the criticism it
deserves.

10     *condemn'd to have* : criticized for
having.
    *an itching palm* : a hand willing
to be rubbed—i.e. to take bribes.

11     *mart* : trade.
    *offices* : official positions.

12     *undeservers* : men who are not
worthy.

14     *else* : otherwise.

15–16     Your name protects this racket,
and only because of this ('therefore')
is there no punishment for it.

20–1     Was there anyone so villainous
as to stab Caesar for some other reason
than the cause of justice?

23     *But . . . robbers* : for the very
reason that he allowed robbers to go
unpunished.

26     *trash* : rubbish.
    *thus*. Perhaps Brutus clenches his
fist to show a hand grasping money.

27     *bay* : howl at.

28     *bait* : try to anger.

29–30     *you . . . in* : you forget who you
are, when you try to bind me with your
rules.

31     *older in practice* : more
experienced in practical matters.

32     *make conditions* : manage affairs.
    *Go to* : nonsense.

35     *Urge* : tempt.

36     *Have . . . health* : think of what
is good for you.

39     Must I submit ('give way and

**Cassius**                I an itching palm!
You know that you are Brutus that speak this,
Or, by the gods, this speech were else your last.

**Brutus**
15 The name of Cassius honours this corruption,
And chastisement doth therefore hide his head.

**Cassius**
Chastisement!

**Brutus**
Remember March, the ides of March remember:
Did not great Julius bleed for justice' sake?
20 What villain touch'd his body, that did stab,
And not for justice? What, shall one of us,
That struck the foremost man of all this world
But for supporting robbers, shall we now
Contaminate our fingers with base bribes,
25 And sell the mighty space of our large honours
For so much trash as may be grasped thus?
I had rather be a dog, and bay the moon,
Than such a Roman.

**Cassius**            Brutus, bait not me;
I'll not endure it: you forget yourself,
30 To hedge me in. I am a soldier, I,
Older in practice, abler than yourself
To make conditions.

**Brutus**           Go to; you are not, Cassius.

**Cassius**
I am.

**Brutus**
I say you are not.

**Cassius**
35 Urge me no more, I shall forget myself;
Have mind upon your health; tempt me no further.

**Brutus**
Away, slight man!

**Cassius**
Is 't possible?

**Brutus**           Hear me, for I will speak.
Must I give way and room to your rash choler?
40 Shall I be frighted when a madman stares?

**Cassius**
O ye gods! ye gods! Must I endure all this?

room') to your quick temper ('rash choler')?

42    *fret :* rage.

44    *budge :* change my position.
45    *observe :* take notice of.
46    *testy humour :* irritable temper.
47-8  *You . . . split you :* you can swallow the poison of your anger ('spleen') even if you burst with it.

48    *forth :* onwards.
49    *mirth :* amusement.
50    *waspish :* bad-tempered.

52    *Let . . . so :* let me see it.
       *vaunting :* boasting.
53    *mine own part :* myself.

58    *durst :* dare.
       *mov'd :* angered.

63    *presume :* take advantage.

67    My honesty is like a strong armour.
68    *they :* i.e. the threats.
69    *respect not :* take no notice of.
       *send to you :* sent to ask you.

**Brutus**
All this? ay, more: fret till your proud heart break;
Go show your slaves how choleric you are,
And make your bondmen tremble. Must I budge?
45 Must I observe you? Must I stand and crouch
Under your testy humour? By the gods,
You shall digest the venom of your spleen,
Though it do split you; for, from this day forth,
I'll use you for my mirth, yea, for my laughter,
50 When you are waspish.
           **Cassius**   *disappoint*        Is it come to this?
           **Brutus**
You say you are a better soldier:
Let it appear so; make your vaunting true,
And it shall please me well. For mine own part,
I shall be glad to learn of noble men.
           **Cassius**
55 You wrong me every way; you wrong me, Brutus;
I said an elder soldier, not a better:
Did I say, 'better'?
           **Brutus**              If you did, I care not.
           **Cassius**
When Caesar liv'd, he durst not thus have mov'd me.
           **Brutus**
Peace, peace! you durst not so have tempted him.
           **Cassius**
60 I durst not?
           **Brutus**
No.
           **Cassius**
What! durst not tempt him?
           **Brutus**           For your life you durst not.
           **Cassius**
Do not presume too much upon my love;
I may do that I shall be sorry for.
           **Brutus**
65 You have done that you should be sorry for.
There is no terror, Cassius, in your threats;
For I am arm'd so strong in honesty
That they pass by me as the idle wind,
Which I respect not. I did send to you
70 For certain sums of gold, which you denied me;

71      *vile :* dishonourable.
72-5    I would rather turn my heart into
        gold and my drops of blood into silver
        coins ('drachmas') than squeeze the
        hardworking (and unwilling) hands
        of the peasants to get their poor money
76      *legions :* detachments of troops.

80      *rascal counters :* wretched bits of
metal.

84      *riv'd :* torn.

85      *bear :* accept.
        *infirmities :* weaknesses.

87      *practise :* use.

91      *Olympus :* the mountain home of
the Greek gods.

93      *alone :* only.

95      *brav'd :* defied.
96      *Check'd :* corrected.
97      *conn'd by rote :* learned by heart.
98      *To . . . teeth :* to repeat to my face.
98-9    *weep . . . eyes :* die of grief.

101     *Pluto :* the god of the underworld,
but often confused (as here) with
Plutus, god of riches.

For I can raise no money by vile means:
By heaven, I had rather coin my heart,
And drop my blood for drachmas, than to wring
From the hard hands of peasants their vile trash
By any indirection. I did send                                  75
To you for gold to pay my legions,
Which you denied me: was that done like Cassius?
Should I have answer'd Caius Cassius so?
When Marcus Brutus grows so covetous,
To lock such rascal counters from his friends,             80
Be ready, gods, with all your thunderbolts;
Dash him to pieces!
                Cassius                    I denied you not.
                Brutus
You did.
                Cassius             I did not: he was but a fool
That brought my answer back. Brutus hath riv'd
my heart.
A friend should bear his friend's infirmities,             85
But Brutus makes mine greater than they are.
                Brutus
I do not, till you practise them on me.
                Cassius
You love me not.
                Brutus              I do not like your faults.
                Cassius
A friendly eye could never see such faults.
                Brutus
A flatterer's would not, though they do appear         90
As huge as high Olympus.
                Cassius
Come, Antony, and young Octavius, come,
Revenge yourselves alone on Cassius,
For Cassius is aweary of the world:
Hated by one he loves; brav'd by his brother;            95
Check'd like a bondman; all his faults observ'd,
Set in a note-book, learn'd, and conn'd by rote,
To cast into my teeth. O, I could weep
My spirit from mine eyes. There is my dagger,
And here my naked breast; within, a heart                  100
Dearer than Pluto's mine, richer than gold:
If that thou be'st a Roman, take it forth;
I, that denied thee gold, will give my heart:
Strike, as thou didst at Caesar; for, I know,

105 When thou didst hate him worst, thou lov'dst him
        better
Than ever thou lov'dst Cassius.
        **Brutus**                     Sheathe your dagger:
Be angry when you will, it shall have scope;
Do what you will, dishonour shall be humour.
O Cassius, you are yoked with a lamb
110 That carries anger as the flint bears fire,
Who, much enforced, shows a hasty spark,
And straight is cold again.
        **Cassius**                     Hath Cassius liv'd
To be but mirth and laughter to his Brutus,
When grief and blood ill-temper'd vexeth him?
        **Brutus**
115 When I spoke that I was ill-temper'd too.
        **Cassius**
Do you confess so much? Give me your hand.
        **Brutus**
And my heart too.
        **Cassius**          O Brutus!
        **Brutus**                     What's the matter?
        **Cassius**
Have not you love enough to bear with me,
When that rash humour which my mother gave me
120 Makes me forgetful?
        **Brutus**      Yes, Cassius; and from henceforth
When you are over-earnest with your Brutus,
He'll think your mother chides, and leave you so.
                                    [*Noise within*
        **Poet**
[*Within*] Let me go in to see the generals;
There is some grudge between 'em, 'tis not meet
125 They be alone.
        **Lucilius**
[*Within*] You shall not come to them.
        **Poet**
[*Within*] Nothing but death shall stay me.

            *Enter* Poet, *followed by* Lucilius, Titinius,
            *and* Lucius
        **Cassius**
Now now! What's the matter?
        **Poet**
For shame, you generals! What do you mean?

---

107    *scope :* free expression.
108    *dishonour . . . humour :* when you
    insult me, I will think that you are
    only in a mood.
109    *yoked :* allied.
110-12  Brutus says that in his anger he
    is like a flint that does not give fire
    until it has been struck repeatedly and
    with violence ('much enforced'); then
    it gives a brief ('hasty') spark, and is
    immediately ('straight') cold again.
114    *blood ill-temper'd :* ill humour.

116    *confess :* admit.

118    *bear :* be patient.
119    *that . . . me :* that quick temper
    that I was born with.
120    *forgetful :* forget myself.

121    *over-earnest :* too hard on.
122    *chides :* is angry.
    *leave you so :* leave it at that.

124    *grudge :* quarrel.
    *meet :* right.

130 Love, and be friends, as two such men should be;
For I have seen more years, I'm sure, than ye.
    **Cassius**

132    *cynic :* would-be philosopher.

Ha, ha! how vilely doth this cynic rhyme!
    **Brutus**
Get you hence, sirrah; saucy fellow, hence!
    **Cassius**

134    *'tis his fashion :* it's just his way.

Bear with him, Brutus, 'tis his fashion.
    **Brutus**

135    I'll make allowances ('know') for
his manner ('humour') when he
recognizes that there is a proper time
for it.

135 I'll know his humour, when he knows his time.
What should the wars do with these jigging fools?

136    What use are these rhyming
('jigging') fools in time of war?

Companion, hence!
    **Cassius**               Away, away! be gone.
                                    [*Exit* Poet

137    *Companion :* fellow.

    **Brutus**
Lucilius and Titinius, bid the commanders

139    *lodge :* pitch camp for.

Prepare to lodge their companies tonight.
    **Cassius**
140 And come yourselves, and bring Messala with you,
Immediately to us.
                          [*Exeunt* Lucilius *and* Titinius
    **Brutus**                  Lucius, a bowl of wine!
                                        [*Exit* Lucius
    **Cassius**
I did not think you could have been so angry.
    **Brutus**
O Cassius, I am sick of many griefs.
    **Cassius**

143    *sick :* weary.
    *griefs :* problems.

Of your philosophy you make no use

144-5    You are not being very
philosophical (see p. 99) if you give
in to difficulties that only happen by
chance ('accidental').

145 If you give place to accidental evils.
    **Brutus**
No man bears sorrow better. Portia is dead.
    **Cassius**
Ha? Portia?
    **Brutus**
She is dead.
    **Cassius**

149    *'scap'd :* escaped.
    *cross'd :* angered.

How 'scap'd I killing when I cross'd you so?

150    The loss of someone very close to
('touching') you is unbearable
('insupportable').

150 O insupportable and touching loss!
Upon what sickness?

151    *Upon :* of.
    *Impatient :* unable to endure.

    **Brutus**             Impatient of my absence,
And grief that young Octavius with Mark Antony

153-4    *for . . . came :* the news of her

Have made themselves so strong—for with her

**154** *fell distract :* went out of her mind.

**155** *her . . . absent :* when her attendants had left her alone.
*swallow'd fire.* Portia committed suicide by filling her mouth with burning coals and keeping her lips together.

**156sd** *tapers :* candles.

**158** I will drown all the bad feeling ('unkindness') between us in this wine.

**160** *o'erswell :* overflows.

**164** Ask ourselves what needs to be done.

**168** *Come . . . us :* are advancing towards us.
**169** *Bending :* directing.
*expedition :* rapid movement.
**170** *of . . . tenor :* to the same effect.

**171** With anything else.

**172** *proscription :* condemning to death.
*bills of outlawry :* sentencing to exile.

---

death came together with that other news.

death
That tidings came—with this she fell distract,
**155** And, her attendants absent, swallow'd fire.
**Cassius**
And died so?
**Brutus**      Even so.
**Cassius**                    O ye immortal gods!

*Enter* Lucius, *with wine and tapers*
**Brutus**
Speak no more of her. Give me a bowl of wine.
In this I bury all unkindness, Cassius.      [*Drinks*
**Cassius**
My heart is thirsty for that noble pledge.
**160** Fill, Lucius, till the wine o'erswell the cup;
I cannot drink too much of Brutus' love.   [*Drinks*
**Brutus**
Come in, Titinius.      [*Exit* Lucius

*Enter* Titinius *and* Messala
                    Welcome, good Messala.
Now sit we close about this taper here,
And call in question our necessities.
**Cassius**
**165** Portia, art thou gone?
**Brutus**                    No more, I pray you.
Messala, I have here received letters,
That young Octavius and Mark Antony
Come down upon us with a mighty power,
Bending their expedition towards Philippi.
**Messala**
**170** Myself have letters of the self-same tenor.
**Brutus**
With what addition?
**Messala**
That by proscription and bills of outlawry,
Octavius, Antony, and Lepidus
Have put to death an hundred senators.
**Brutus**
**175** Therein our letters do not well agree;
Mine speak of seventy senators that died
By their proscriptions, Cicero being one.
**Cassius**
Cicero one!

180    *Had . . . wife :* were your letters
from your wife?
180–94  See p. xxii.

182    *writ of :* written about.

184    *aught :* anything.

190    When I think that she must die
at some time ('once').

192    *Even so :* this is just the way.

193    *art :* theory.

195    *to . . . alive :* let us get on with the
business of living.

199    *waste :* exhaust.
       *means :* supplies.
200    *Doing himself offence :* harming
himself.
       *lying still :* staying in the same
place.
202    *of force :* necessarily.
204    Are only friendly towards us
because they are compelled ('forc'd')
to be.
205    *grudg'd us contribution :* been
unwilling to supply us.

**Messala**                        Cicero is dead,
And by that order of proscription.
180 [Had you your letters from your wife, my lord?
       **Brutus**
No, Messala.
       **Messala**
Nor nothing in your letters writ of her?
       **Brutus**
Nothing, Messala.
       **Messala**                That, methinks, is strange.
       **Brutus**
Why ask you? Hear you aught of her in yours?
       **Messala**
185 No, my lord.
       **Brutus**
Now, as you are a Roman, tell me true.
       **Messala**
Then like a Roman bear the truth I tell:
For certain she is dead, and by strange manner.
       **Brutus**
Why, farewell, Portia. We must die, Messala:
190 With meditating that she must die once,
I have the patience to endure it now.
       **Messala**
Even so great men great losses should endure.
       **Cassius**
I have as much of this in art as you,
But yet my nature could not bear it so.]
       **Brutus**
195 Well, to our work alive. What do you think
Of marching to Philippi presently?
       **Cassius**
I do not think it good.
       **Brutus**                Your reason?
       **Cassius**                        This is it:
'Tis better that the enemy seek us;
So shall he waste his means, weary his soldiers,
200 Doing himself offence; whilst we, lying still,
Are full of rest, defence, and nimbleness.
       **Brutus**
Good reasons must, of force, give place to better.
The people 'twixt Philippi and this ground
Do stand but in a forc'd affection;
205 For they have grudg'd us contribution.

206 *by them*: through their land.
207 *By them*: from them.
    *make . . . up*: increase the size of
    his army.
208 *Come on*: advance.
    *new-added*: reinforced.

213 *tried . . . friends*: we have asked
    our allies for all the help they can give.
214 *Our . . . brim-full*: our armies are
    as large as they need to be.
    *our . . . ripe*: this is the right
    moment to fight for our cause.
216 *at the height*: i.e. of strength and
    fortune.
218 *flood*: high tide.
219 *Omitted*: if men fail to take the
    opportunity presented to them.
220 *bound in shallows*: stranded in
    shallow water.
222 *serves*: is best for us.
223 *ventures*: enterprises (goods
    risked in trade).
    *with*: at.
225 It has got late into the night
    whilst we have been talking.
226-7 Human nature must admit its
    needs, and we will satisfy these needs
    with a short rest ('niggard' = be
    sparing, or mean, with).

230 *gown*: dressing-gown.

The enemy, marching along by them,
By them shall make a fuller number up,
Come on refresh'd, new-added, and encourag'd;
From which advantage shall we cut him off
210 If at Philippi we do face him there,
These people at our back.
  **Cassius**     Hear me, good brother.
  **Brutus**
Under your pardon. You must note beside,
That we have tried the utmost of our friends,
Our legions are brim-full, our cause is ripe.
215 The enemy increaseth every day;
We, at the height, are ready to decline.
There is a tide in the affairs of men,
Which, taken at the flood, leads on to fortune;
Omitted, all the voyage of their life
220 Is bound in shallows and in miseries.
On such a full sea are we now afloat,
And we must take the current when it serves,
Or lose our ventures.
  **Cassius**   Then, with your will, go on;
We'll along ourselves, and meet them at Philippi.
  **Brutus**
225 The deep of night is crept upon our talk,
And nature must obey necessity,
Which we will niggard with a little rest.
There is no more to say?
  **Cassius**     No more. Good-night:
Early tomorrow will we rise, and hence.
  **Brutus**
230 Lucius!

    *Enter* Lucius
   My gown.     [*Exit* Lucius
         Farewell, good Messala.
Good-night, Titinius. Noble, noble Cassius,
Good-night, and good repose.
  **Cassius**    O my dear brother,
This was an ill beginning of the night:
Never come such division 'tween our souls!
235 Let it not, Brutus.
  **Brutus**     Every thing is well.
  **Cassius**
Good-night, my lord.

**Brutus**                Good-night, good brother.
**Titinius** } Good-night, Lord Brutus.
**Messala**
**Brutus**                        Farewell, every one.
                    [*Exeunt* Cassius, Titinius, *and* Messala

                *Enter* Lucius, *with the gown*
Give me the gown. Where is thy instrument?
    **Lucius**
Here in the tent.
    **Brutus**                What, thou speak'st drowsily
240 Poor knave, I blame thee not; thou art o'er-watch'd,
Call Claudius and some other of my men;
I'll have them sleep on cushions in my tent.
    **Lucius**
Varro and Claudius!

                *Enter* Varro *and* Claudius
    **Varro**
Calls my lord?
    **Brutus**
245 I pray you, sirs, lie in my tent and sleep:
It may be I shall raise you by and by
On business to my brother Cassius.
    **Varro**
So please you, we will stand and watch your
    pleasure.
    **Brutus**
I will not have it so; lie down, good sirs;
250 It may be I shall otherwise bethink me.
                        [Varro *and* Claudius *lie down*
Look, Lucius, here's the book I sought for so;
I put it in the pocket of my gown.
    **Lucius**
I was sure your lordship did not give it me.
    **Brutus**
Bear with me, good boy, I am much forgetful.
255 Canst thou hold up thy heavy eyes awhile,
And touch thy instrument a strain or two?
    **Lucius**
Ay, my lord, an 't please you.
    **Brutus**                It does, my boy:
I trouble thee too much, but thou art willing.

240    *art o'er-watch'd :* have been kept
    awake too long.

246    *raise :* rouse.
247    *On business :* to go on business.
248    *watch your pleasure :* stay awake
    until you need us.
250    *otherwise bethink me :* decide to
    do something else.

256    *touch . . . two :* play one or two
    tunes on your instrument (probably
    a lute).
257    *an 't :* if it.

**Lucius**
It is my duty, sir.
**Brutus**
260 I should not urge thy duty past thy might;
I know young bloods look for a time of rest.
**Lucius**
I have slept, my lord, already.
**Brutus**
It was well done, and thou shalt sleep again;
I will not hold thee long: if I do live,
265 I will be good to thee.        [*Music, and a Song*
This is a sleepy tune: O murd'rous slumber!
Lay'st thou thy leaden mace upon my boy,
That plays thee music? Gentle knave, good-night;
I will not do thee so much wrong to wake thee.
270 If thou dost nod, thou break'st thy instrument;
I'll take it from thee; and, good boy, good-night.
Let me see, let me see; is not the leaf turn'd down
Where I left reading? Here it is, I think.

*Enter the Ghost of* Caesar
How ill this taper burns! Ha! who comes here?
275 I think it is the weakness of mine eyes
That shapes this monstrous apparition.
It comes upon me. Art thou any thing?
Art thou some god, some angel, or some devil,
That mak'st my blood cold and my hair to stare?
280 Speak to me what thou art.
**Ghost**
Thy evil spirit, Brutus.
**Brutus**                    Why com'st thou?
**Ghost**
To tell thee thou shalt see me at Philippi.
**Brutus**
Well; then I shall see thee again?
**Ghost**                    Ay, at Philippi.
**Brutus**
Why, I will see thee at Philippi then.
                        [*Exit Ghost*
285 Now I have taken heart thou vanishest:
Ill spirit, I would hold more talk with thee.
Boy! Lucius! Varro! Claudius! Sirs, awake!
Claudius!
**Lucius**
The strings, my lord, are false.

---

261  *bloods*: constitutions.
    *look for*: need.

264  *hold*: keep.

267  *leaden*: heavy (made of lead).
    *mace.* Officers arresting wrong-doers carried a mace, with which they touched the criminal on the shoulder as a token of arrest; Shakespeare often personifies death and sleep as arresting officers.
268  *plays thee music.* Brutus thinks of Lucius's playing, intended to lull him to sleep, as a serenade to the personification of sleep.
    *knave*: boy (the tone is affectionate).
274  *How . . . burns.* Elizabethan superstition believed that a candle ('taper') would burn blue if a ghost approached.
277  *upon*: towards.
    *any thing*: i.e. real.
279  *stare*: stand on end.
280  *Speak to*: tell.

285  *taken heart*: recovered my courage; ghosts (the Elizabethans believed) would disappear when they were challenged.
286  *would hold*: would like to have.

289  *false*: out of tune.

**Brutus**
290 He thinks he still is at his instrument.
Lucius, awake!
**Lucius**
My lord!
**Brutus**
Didst thou dream, Lucius, that thou so criedst out?
**Lucius**
My lord, I do not know that I did cry.
**Brutus**
295 Yes, that thou didst. Didst thou see any thing?
**Lucius**
Nothing, my lord.
**Brutus**
Sleep again, Lucius. Sirrah, Claudius!
Fellow thou! awake!
**Varro**
My lord?
**Claudius**
300 My lord?
**Brutus**
Why did you so cry out, sirs, in your sleep?
**Varro**
**Claudius** } Did we, my lord?
**Brutus**                    Ay: saw you any thing?
**Varro**
No, my lord, I saw nothing.
**Claudius**                   Nor I, my lord.
**Brutus**
Go, and commend me to my brother Cassius.
305 Bid him set on his powers betimes before,
And we will follow.
**Varro**
**Claudius** } It shall be done, my lord.
                                      [*Exeunt*

304     *commend me :* present my
    compliments to.
305     *set on his powers :* order his
    troops to advance.
        *betimes :* early.
        *before :* i.e. before my soldiers.

# Act 5

**Act 5   Scene 1**

Antony and Octavius face the rebel
army. Antony rebukes Brutus for the
murder of Caesar, and then withdraws
to prepare for battle. Cassius is uneasy,
and tells Messala of omens he has
noticed which suggest that the rebels
will be unsuccessful. Cassius and
Brutus are both resolved to die rather
than be taken prisoner. Plutarch's
version of this last episode is given
on p. 99.

1     *answered*: fulfilled (Octavius is
being ironic; the opposite of what they
hoped for has happened).

3     *keep*: remain in.

4     *battles*: armies.

5     *warn*: challenge.

6     Responding to our challenge
before it is made.

7     *Tut*: don't worry.
    *am . . . bosoms*: know what is in
their hearts.

8-9     *could . . . places*: would prefer
to be somewhere else.

10     *fearful bravery*: a show of
splendour ('bravery') that is full of fear.
    *face*: appearance.

11     *fasten . . . thoughts*: give us the
impression.

13     *in gallant show*: with a splendid
appearance.

14     *bloody . . . battle*: red flag (the
Roman signal for battle).

15     *something . . . done*: some action
is to be taken.

16     *battle*: forces.
    *softly*: steadily.

17     *even field*: level ground.

18     *right hand*. This was the more
honourable side.

19     *cross*: oppose.
    *exigent*: decision.

**Scene 1** *Philippi: the plains*

> *Enter* Octavius, Antony, *and their Army*

**Octavius**
Now, Antony, our hopes are answered!
You said the enemy would not come down,
But keep the hills and upper regions.
It proves not so; their battles are at hand;
5 They mean to warn us at Philippi here,
Answering before we do demand of them.

**Antony**
Tut! I am in their bosoms, and I know
Wherefore they do it: they could be content
To visit other places, and come down
10 With fearful bravery, thinking by this face
To fasten in our thoughts that they have courage;
But 'tis not so.

> *Enter a* Messenger

**Messenger**          Prepare you, generals:
The enemy comes on in gallant show;
Their bloody sign of battle is hung out,
15 And something to be done immediately.

**Antony**
Octavius, lead your battle softly on,
Upon the left hand of the even field.

**Octavius**
Upon the right hand I; keep thou the left.

**Antony**
Why do you cross me in this exigent?

**Octavius**
20 I do not cross you; but I will do so.    *[March*

> *Drum. Enter* Brutus, Cassius, Lucilius,
> Titinius, Messala, *and their Army*

**Brutus**
They stand, and would have parley.

21   They are stopping and asking for
a conference.

**Cassius**
22   *Stand fast :* halt.
Stand fast, Titinius; we must out and talk.

**Octavius**
Mark Antony, shall we give sign of battle?

**Antony**
24   *charge :* attack.
No, Caesar, we will answer on their charge.

25   *Make forth :* go forward.
25 Make forth; the generals would have some words.

**Octavius**
Stir not until the signal.

**Brutus**
Words before blows: is it so, countrymen?

**Octavius**
Not that we love words better, as you do.

**Brutus**
Good words are better than bad strokes, Octavius.

**Antony**
30 In your bad strokes, Brutus, you give good words:

31   *Witness :* as can be seen from.
Witness the hole you made in Caesar's heart,
Crying, 'Long live! hail, Caesar!'

**Cassius**                              Antony,

33   *posture . . . blows :* what kind of
blows you can strike.
The posture of your blows are yet unknown;

34   *Hybla :* a mountain in Sicily,
famous for its honey.
But for your words, they rob the Hybla bees,
35 And leave them honeyless.

**Antony**                              Not stingless too?

**Brutus**
O yes, and soundless too;
For you have stol'n their buzzing, Antony,

38   *threat :* threaten.
And very wisely threat before you sting.

**Antony**

39   *so :* i.e. threaten before they
stabbed Caesar.
Villains! you did not so when your vile daggers
40 Hack'd one another in the sides of Caesar:

41   *show'd your teeth :* grinned.
You show'd your teeth like apes, and fawn'd like
    hounds,
And bow'd like bondmen, kissing Caesar's feet;
Whilst damned Casca, like a cur, behind
Struck Caesar on the neck. O you flatterers!

**Cassius**

45   *thank yourself :* you have only
yourself to thank (for this insult).
45 Flatterers! Now, Brutus, thank yourself:
This tongue had not offended so today,

47   *rul'd :* had his way.
If Cassius might have rul'd.

48    *cause* : come to the point.
49    *proof* : deciding the argument in battle.
      *redder drops* : drops of red blood (not drops of sweat).
52    *goes up* : is sheathed.

54    *another Caesar* : i.e. himself.
55    Has increased the slaughter done by traitors.

57    *Unless . . . thee* : unless they are on your side (Brutus maintains his, and the rebels', loyalty to Rome).
      *So I hope* : i.e. that I shall not be killed by a traitor—one on Brutus's side.
59    *strain* : family.

61    *peevish* : sulky.
62    *masker* : one who wears a mask at parties.

66    *stomachs* : appetites for fighting.

67    *swim bark* : let the ship sail (i.e. whatever happens, we must fight).
68    *on the hazard* : at risk.

74    *Pompey*. At the battle of Pharsalia Pompey was compelled to fight against his better judgement; he was defeated.
      *set* : risk.
76-7  *I held . . . opinion* : used to believe firmly in Epicurus (a Greek philosopher) and his view (that omens were not to be trusted because they were mere superstition).

**Octavius**
Come, come, the cause: if arguing make us sweat,
The proof of it will turn to redder drops.
50 Look;
I draw a sword against conspirators;
When think you that the sword goes up again?
Never, till Caesar's three-and-thirty wounds
Be well aveng'd; or till another Caesar
55 Have added slaughter to the sword of traitors.
**Brutus**
Caesar, thou canst not die by traitors' hands,
Unless thou bring'st them with thee.
**Octavius**                                    So I hope;
I was not born to die on Brutus' sword.
**Brutus**
O, if thou wert the noblest of thy strain,
60 Young man, thou couldst not die more honourable.
**Cassius**
A peevish schoolboy, worthless of such honour,
Join'd with a masker and a reveller.
**Antony**
Old Cassius still!
**Octavius**                          Come, Antony; away!
Defiance, traitors, hurl we in your teeth.
65 If you dare fight today, come to the field;
If not, when you have stomachs.
            [*Exeunt* Octavius, Antony, *and their Army*
**Cassius**
Why now, blow wind, swell billow, and swim bark!
The storm is up, and all is on the hazard.
**Brutus**
Ho! Lucilius hark, a word with you.
**Lucilius**                                    My lord?
            [Brutus *and* Lucilius *talk apart*
**Cassius**
70 Messala!
**Messala**   What says my general?
**Cassius**                                    Messala,
This is my birthday; as this very day
Was Cassius born. Give me thy hand, Messala:
Be thou my witness that against my will,
(As Pompey was) am I compell'd to set
75 Upon one battle all our liberties.
You know that I held Epicurus strong,
And his opinion; now I change my mind,

| | |
|---|---|
| 78 | *credit . . . presage :* believe in things that foretell the future. |
| 79 | *former :* foremost. |
| | *ensign :* standard. |
| 80 | *fell :* alighted. |
| 82 | *consorted :* accompanied. |
| 84 | *stead :* place. |
| 86 | *As :* as if. |
| | *sickly :* i.e. likely to die. |
| 87 | *fatal :* signifying death (like the canopy over a bier). |
| 88 | *give . . . ghost :* die. |
| 89 | *but . . . partly :* only half-believe it. |
| 90 | *fresh of spirit :* hopeful in my mind. |
| 91 | *constantly :* with courage. |
| 92 | *Even so :* that's all (Brutus finishes his conversation with Lucilius). |
| 93 | *The . . . friendly :* may the gods be on our side. |
| 94 | *Lovers :* good friends. |
| | *lead . . . age :* live to old age. |
| 95 | *rests :* remain. |
| | *still :* always. |
| 96 | Let's decide what to do if the worst happens. |
| 100–2 | I shall act according to the principles of that philosophy (Stoicism) which made me censure Cato (Portia's father) for killing himself (see note on *2, 1, 295*). Stoicism taught that suicide was 'cowardly and vile'; men should endure all suffering with patience and fortitude. |
| 104–5 | *For . . . life :* to anticipate |

And partly credit things that do presage.
Coming from Sardis, on our former ensign
80 Two mighty eagles fell, and there they perch'd,
Gorging and feeding from our soldiers' hands,
Who to Philippi here consorted us.
This morning are they fled away and gone,
And in their stead do ravens, crows, and kites
85 Fly o'er our heads, and downward look on us,
As we were sickly prey: their shadows seem
A canopy most fatal, under which
Our army lies, ready to give up the ghost.
    **Messala**
Believe not so.
    **Cassius**              I but believe it partly,
90 For I am fresh of spirit and resolv'd
To meet all perils very constantly.
    **Brutus**
Even so, Lucilius.
    **Cassius**             Now, most noble Brutus,
The gods today stand friendly, that we may,
Lovers in peace, lead on our days to age!
95 But since the affairs of men rests still incertain,
Let's reason with the worst that may befall.
If we do lose this battle, then is this
The very last time we shall speak together:
What are you, then, determined to do?
    **Brutus**
100 Even by the rule of that philosophy
By which I did blame Cato for the death
Which he did give himself. I know not how,
But I do find it cowardly and vile,
For fear of what might fall, so to prevent

('prevent') the natural end of life because one is afraid of what might happen.

105  *arming* : fortifying.
106  *stay* : wait.
106–7  *the . . . below* : the destiny ordained by the gods who rule men on earth.
108–9  The Romans led their prisoners of war in procession ('triumph') through ('Thorough') the streets of Rome.
111  *bound* : as a prisoner.

115  *everlasting* : final.

105  The time of life, arming myself with patience,
To stay the providence of some high powers
That govern us below.

**Cassius**                    Then, if we lose this battle,
You are contented to be led in triumph
Thorough the streets of Rome?

**Brutus**

110  No, Cassius, no: think not, thou noble Roman,
That ever Brutus will go bound to Rome;
He bears too great a mind. But this same day
Must end that work the ides of March begun;
And whether we shall meet again I know not.

115  Therefore our everlasting farewell take:
For ever, and for ever, farewell, Cassius.
If we do meet again, why, we shall smile;
If not, why then, this parting was well made.

**Cassius**

For ever, and for ever, farewell, Brutus.

120  If we do meet again, we'll smile indeed;
If not, 'tis true this parting was well made.

**Brutus**

Why, then, lead on. O, that a man might know
The end of this day's business, ere it come;
But it sufficeth that the day will end,

125  And then the end is known. Come, ho! away!

[*Exeunt*

**Act 5    Scene 2**

Battle has commenced, and Brutus is hopeful.

sd  *Alarum* : trumpet signal for attack.
1  *bills* : written orders.
2  *other side* : i.e. the troops led by Cassius.
3  *set on* : charge.
4  *cold demeanour* : faint courage.
   *wing* : troops.
5  *push* : attack.
   *overthrow* : defeat.

**Scene 2** *Philippi : the battlefield*

*Alarum. Enter* Brutus *and* Messala

**Brutus**

Ride, ride, Messala, ride, and give these bills
Unto the legions on the other side.    [*Loud alarum*
Let them set on at once, for I perceive
But cold demeanour in Octavius' wing,

5  And sudden push gives them the overthrow.
Ride, ride, Messala: let them all come down.

[*Exeunt*

## Act 5   Scene 3

It seems as though Brutus was in too great a hurry, and now Cassius's troops are surrounded by the Roman legions. Cassius sends Pindarus, his slave, to the top of a hill, and when Pindarus reports more disaster, Cassius orders the slave to kill him. But Pindarus was mistaken; Titinius enters with news of success. Finding Cassius dead, Titinius kills himself. Brutus comes to see Cassius's body, and promises to mourn the death of his friend when the battle is over and there is time for grief.

1   *the villains*: i.e. his own men.
2   I have turned against my own men.
3   *ensign*: standard bearer.
4   *it*: i.e. the standard.
6   *on*: over.
7   *fell to spoil*: started to plunder.
8   *all enclos'd*: quite surrounded.
10  *tents*: camp.
11  *far*: further.

15  *hide thy spurs*: dig your spurs in deeply.
17  *rest assur'd*: know.
18  *yond*: yonder.

19  *even . . . thought*: as quick as a thought.

21  *My . . . thick*: I have always been short-sighted.
    *regard*: watch.
22  *not'st*: see.

25  *is run his compass*: has come full circle.

**Scene 3** *Philippi: another part of the battlefield*

*Alarum. Enter* Cassius *and* Titinius

**Cassius**
O look, Titinius, look, the villains fly.
Myself have to mine own turn'd enemy;
This ensign here of mine was turning back;
I slew the coward, and did take it from him.

**Titinius**
5 O Cassius, Brutus gave the word too early;
Who, having some advantage on Octavius,
Took it too eagerly; his soldiers fell to spoil,
Whilst we by Antony are all enclos'd.

*Enter* Pindarus

**Pindarus**
Fly further off, my lord, fly further off!
10 Mark Antony is in your tents, my lord;
Fly, therefore, noble Cassius, fly far off.

**Cassius**
This hill is far enough. Look, look, Titinius;
Are those my tents where I perceive the fire?

**Titinius**
They are, my lord.

**Cassius**              Titinius, if thou lov'st me,
15 Mount thou my horse, and hide thy spurs in him,
Till he have brought thee up to yonder troops
And here again; that I may rest assur'd
Whether yond troops are friend or enemy.

**Titinius**
I will be here again, even with a thought.    [*Exit*

**Cassius**
20 Go, Pindarus, get higher on that hill;
My sight was ever thick; regard Titinius,
And tell me what thou not'st about the field.
                            [*Exit* Pindarus
This day I breathed first; time is come round,
And where I did begin, there shall I end;
25 My life is run his compass. Sirrah, what news?

**Pindarus**
[*Above*] O my lord!

**Cassius**
What news?

Pindarus

Titinius is enclosed round about
With horsemen, that make to him on the spur;
30 Yet he spurs on. Now they are almost on him;
Now, Titinius! now some light; O, he lights too;
He's ta'en; [*Shout*] and, hark! they shout for joy.

Cassius

Come down; behold no more.
O, coward that I am, to live so long,
35 To see my best friend ta'en before my face!

*Enter* Pindarus
Come hither, sirrah.
In Parthia did I take thee prisoner;
And then I swore thee, saving of thy life,
That whatsoever I did bid thee do,
40 Thou shouldst attempt it. Come now, keep thine
        oath;
Now be a freeman; and with this good sword,
That ran through Caesar's bowels, search this
        bosom.
Stand not to answer; here, take thou the hilts;
And, when my face is cover'd, as 'tis now,
45 Guide thou the sword.
            [Pindarus *takes the sword and kills* Cassius
                        Caesar, thou art reveng'd,
Even with the sword that kill'd thee.        [*Dies*

Pindarus

So, I am free; yet would not so have been,
Durst I have done my will. O Cassius!
Far from this country Pindarus shall run,
50 Where never Roman shall take note of him.    [*Exit*

*Enter* Titinius *with* Messala

Messala

It is but change, Titinius; for Octavius
Is overthrown by noble Brutus' power,
As Cassius' legions are by Antony.

Titinius

These tidings will well comfort Cassius.

Messala

55 Where did you leave him?

Titinius                          All disconsolate,
With Pindarus his bondman, on this hill.

---

28    *enclosed* : surrounded.
29    *on the spur* : spurring their
horses.
31        *light* : alight, dismount.

38        *I swore thee* : I made you promise.
*saving of* : because I saved.

41    *be a freeman* : i.e. it will set you
free from slavery.
42        *search* : probe into.
43        *Stand* : wait.
        *hilts* : handle of the sword.

48        *Durst . . . will* : if I had done as
I wished.
50        *take note* : observe.

51        *but change* : only exchange of
fortune (Cassius's army is defeated,
but the troops led by Brutus have been
victorious).

54        *These tidings* : this news.
*well* : greatly.

**Messala**

Is not that he that lies upon the ground?

**Titinius**

He lies not like the living. O my heart!

**Messala**

Is not that he?

**Titinius**          No, this was he, Messala,

60 But Cassius is no more. O setting sun!

As in thy red rays thou dost sink tonight,

So in his red blood Cassius' day is set;

The sun of Rome is set. Our day is gone;

Clouds, dews, and dangers come; our deeds are
    done.

65 Mistrust of my success hath done this deed.

**Messala**

Mistrust of good success hath done this deed.

O hateful error, melancholy's child,

Why dost thou show to the apt thoughts of men

The things that are not? O error, soon conceiv'd,

70 Thou never com'st unto a happy birth,

But kill'st the mother that engender'd thee.

**Titinius**

What, Pindarus! Where art thou, Pindarus?

**Messala**

Seek him, Titinius, whilst I go to meet

The noble Brutus, thrusting this report

75 Into his ears; I may say, thrusting it;

For piercing steel and darts envenomed

Shall be as welcome to the ears of Brutus

As tidings of this sight.

**Titinius**          Hie you, Messala,

And I will seek for Pindarus the while.

[*Exit* Messala

80 Why didst thou send me forth, brave Cassius?

Did I not meet thy friends? and did not they

Put on my brows this wreath of victory,

And bid me give it thee? Didst thou not hear their
    shouts?

Alas, thou hast misconstru'd every thing.

85 But, hold thee, take this garland on thy brow;

Thy Brutus bid me give it thee, and I

Will do his bidding. Brutus, come apace,

And see how I regarded Caius Cassius.

By your leave, gods: this is a Roman's part:

---

64    *dews :* the dew of night.

65    *Mistrust :* doubt.

67    What dreadful mistakes are caused by ('born of') depression.
68    *apt :* willing (to believe the worst).
69    *soon conceiv'd :* quickly imagined.
70-1    There is never a happy result ('birth') from error, which instead kills the parent, depression (by killing the depressed person)—just as a baby, being born, sometimes kills the mother.
71    *engender'd :* gave birth to.

76    *darts envenomed :* poisoned arrows.

78    *Hie :* hasten.

80    *brave :* noble.

82    *wreath of victory :* laurel crown (given to successful warriors).
84    *misconstru'd :* misinterpreted.
85    *hold thee :* wait.
87    *apace :* quickly.
88    *how :* i.e. how highly.
89    *By . . . gods.* Titinius asks pardon from the gods for ending his life prematurely.
    *a Roman's part :* what is expected of a Roman.

90 Come, Cassius' sword, and find Titinius' heart.

[*Kills himself*

*Alarum. Enter* Brutus, Messala, Young
Cato, Strato, Volumnius, *and* Lucilius

**Brutus**

Where, where, Messala, doth his body lie?

**Messala**

Lo, yonder, and Titinius mourning it.

**Brutus**

Titinius' face is upward.

**Cato**                                        He is slain.

**Brutus**

O Julius Caesar, thou art mighty yet!

95 Thy spirit walks abroad, and turns our swords

In our own proper entrails.              [*Alarums*

**Cato**                              Brave Titinius!

Look whe'r he have not crown'd dead Cassius!

**Brutus**

Are yet two Romans living such as these?

The last of all the Romans, fare thee well!

100 It is impossible that ever Rome

Should breed thy fellow. Friends, I owe more tears

To this dead man than you shall see me pay—

I shall find time, Cassius, I shall find time.

Come therefore, and to Thasos send his body:

105 His funerals shall not be in our camp,

Lest it discomfort us. Lucilius, come;

And come, young Cato; let us to the field.

Labeo and Flavius, set our battles on:

'Tis three o'clock; and, Romans, yet ere night

110 We shall try fortune in a second fight.      [*Exeunt*

---

**Scene 4** *Philippi: another part of the field*

*Alarum. Enter fighting,* Soldiers *of both
armies; then* Brutus, Young Cato,
*and* Lucilius

**Brutus**

Yet, countrymen, O yet hold up your heads! [*Exit*

**Cato**

What bastard doth not? Who will go with me?

---

*Left column notes:*

95    *abroad :* at large.

96    *proper :* own; 'own proper' is
repetition for emphasis.

97    *whe'r :* whether, if he hasn't (the
tone is admiring).

98    *yet :* still.

99    *The . . . Romans :* the last man
worthy to be called a Roman.

101    *thy fellow :* a man like you.

105    *funerals :* funeral ceremonies.

106    *discomfort :* dishearten.

107    *field :* battlefield.

108    *set . . . on :* order our troops to
advance.

109    *ere :* before.

110    *try fortune :* try our luck.

**Act 5    Scene 4**

Lucilius is captured by Antony's men,
and he tells them that he is Brutus.
Antony, however, recognizes him.

1    *yet . . . heads :* still fight bravely.

2    *bastard.* Any man who will not
fight bravely cannot be a true Roman.

I will proclaim my name about the field:
I am the son of Marcus Cato, ho!
5 A foe to tyrants, and my country's friend.
I am the son of Marcus Cato, ho!

**Lucilius**

And I am Brutus, Marcus Brutus, I!
Brutus, my country's friend; know me for Brutus!
                    [Soldiers *attack.* Young Cato *is over-
                    powered, and falls*

**Lucilius**

O young and noble Cato, art thou down?
10 Why, now thou diest as bravely as Titinius,
And mayst be honour'd, being Cato's son.

**First Soldier**

Yield, or thou diest.

**Lucilius**                           Only I yield to die:
There is so much that thou wilt kill me straight.
                              [*Offering money*
Kill Brutus, and be honour'd in his death.

**First Soldier**

15 We must not. A noble prisoner!

**Second Soldier**

Room, ho! Tell Antony, Brutus is ta'en.

**First Soldier**

I'll tell the news: here comes the general.

*Enter* Antony

Brutus is ta'en, Brutus is ta'en, my lord.

**Antony**

Where is he?

**Lucilius**

20 Safe, Antony; Brutus is safe enough;
I dare assure thee that no enemy
Shall ever take alive the noble Brutus:
The gods defend him from so great a shame!
When you do find him, or alive or dead,
25 He will be found like Brutus, like himself.

**Antony**

This is not Brutus, friend; but, I assure you,
A prize no less in worth. Keep this man safe,
Give him all kindness: I had rather have
Such men my friends than enemies. Go on,
30 And see whe'r Brutus be alive or dead;
And bring us word unto Octavius' tent,

---

4        *Cato.* See note to 2, 1, 295.

12       *Only . . . die :* I yield only on
condition that you kill me.

13       *straight :* at once.

14       *in his death :* for killing him.

16       *Room, ho :* make way.

24       *or . . . or :* either . . . or.
25       *like himself :* true to his own
nature.

30       *whe'r :* whether.

32    *is chanc'd* : has turned out.

How every thing is chanc'd              [*Exeunt*

**Act 5    Scene 5**

The rebels are defeated, and Brutus chooses to die rather than be captured. When the fighting is over, Antony speaks in praise of Brutus. See p. 100.

**Scene 5** *Philippi : another part of the field*

> *Enter* Brutus, Dardanius, Clitus, Strato, *and* Volumnius

1      *remains* : survivors.

**Brutus**
Come, poor remains of friends, rest on this rock.

2      *Statilius* : He had gone to another part of the field and held up a torch to indicate that all was well there.
3      *or . . . or* : either . . . or.
4      *the word* : the right word.
5      *a deed in fashion* : everyone is being killed now.

**Clitus**
Statilius show'd the torch-light; but, my lord,
He came not back: he is or ta'en or slain.
**Brutus**
Sit thee down, Clitus. Slaying is the word;
5  It is a deed in fashion. Hark thee, Clitus.
                                      [*Whispers*
**Clitus**
What, I, my lord? No, not for all the world.
**Brutus**
Peace, then! no words.
**Clitus**                    I'll rather kill myself.
**Brutus**
Hark thee, Dardanius.           [*Whispers*
**Dardanius**            Shall I do such a deed?
**Clitus**
O, Dardanius!
**Dardanius**
10  O, Clitus!

11     *ill* : bad.

**Clitus**
What ill request did Brutus make to thee?
**Dardanius**
To kill him, Clitus. Look, he meditates.
**Clitus**

13-14  Brutus is like a fine drinking-vessel full to overflowing.

Now is that noble vessel full of grief,
That it runs over even at his eyes.
**Brutus**

15     *list* : listen.

15  Come hither, good Volumnius: list a word.
**Volumnius**
What says my lord?
**Brutus**                    Why this, Volumnius:
The ghost of Caesar hath appear'd to me

18     *several* : separate.

Two several times by night: at Sardis once,
And this last night here in Philippi fields.

20     *hour* : time to die.

20  I know my hour is come.
**Volumnius**                    Not so, my lord.

22      *the world . . . goes :* how things
        have turned out.
23      *pit :* where animals are trapped
        after they have been hunted.
24      *worthy :* honourable.
25      *tarry :* wait.
27      For the sake of that old friend-
        ship, I ask you.
28      *hilts :* handle.
29      *office :* task.
29sd    *Alarum still :* the battle sound
        continues.
30      *tarrying :* lingering.

34      *joy :* rejoice.
35      *no man . . . me :* no man who was
        not faithful to me.
36-8    I shall have more glory in this
        defeat than Octavius and Antony will
        have for their shameful victory.

40      *his :* its.
41-2    My eyes are heavy with sleep,
        and my body needs rest, having
        struggled for nothing else but to reach
        this hour of death.

45      *respect :* reputation.
46      *smatch :* touch.

51      *with . . . will :* half as willingly.

**Brutus**
Nay, I am sure it is, Volumnius.
Thou seest the world, Volumnius, how it goes;
Our enemies have beat us to the pit:      [*Alarum*
It is more worthy to leap in ourselves,
25 Than tarry till they push us. Good Volumnius,
Thou know'st that we two went to school together;
Even for that our love of old, I prithee,
Hold thou my sword-hilts, whilst I run on it.
**Volumnius**
That's not an office for a friend, my lord.
                              [*Alarum still*
**Clitus**
30 Fly, fly, my lord! there is no tarrying here.
**Brutus**
Farewell to you; and you; and you, Volumnius.
Strato, thou hast been all this while asleep;
Farewell to thee too, Strato. Countrymen,
My heart doth joy that yet, in all my life,
35 I found no man but he was true to me.
I shall have glory by this losing day,
More than Octavius and Mark Antony
By this vile conquest shall attain unto.
So fare you well at once; for Brutus' tongue
40 Hath almost ended his life's history:
Night hangs upon mine eyes; my bones would rest,
That have but labour'd to attain this hour.
              [*Alarum. Cry within*, 'Fly, fly, fly!'
**Clitus**
Fly, my lord, fly.
**Brutus**                    Hence! I will follow.
        [*Exeunt* Clitus, Dardanius, *and* Volumnius
I prithee, Strato, stay thou by thy lord:
45 Thou art a fellow of a good respect;
Thy life hath had some smatch of honour in it.
Hold then my sword, and turn away thy face,
While I do run upon it. Wilt thou, Strato?
**Strato**
Give me your hand first: fare you well, my lord.
**Brutus**
50 Farewell, good Strato.—[*He runs on his sword*]
                              Caesar, now be still;
I kill'd not thee with half so good a will.      [*Dies*

Retreat : trumpet call signalling
the end of the battle.

*Alarum. Retreat. Enter* Octavius, Antony,
Messala, Lucilius, *and* Army

**Octavius**
What man is that?

**Messala**
My master's man. Strato, where is thy master?

**Strato**
Free from the bondage you are in, Messala;

55   make . . . him : burn his body on
a funeral pyre.

55 The conquerors can but make a fire of him;
For Brutus only overcame himself,

56   No-one but Brutus has killed
Brutus.

And no man else hath honour by his death.

**Lucilius**
So Brutus should be found. I thank thee, Brutus,
That thou hast prov'd Lucilius' saying true.

59   Lucilius' *saying*. See 5, 4, 21–2.

**Octavius**

60   entertain : take into my service.

60 All that serv'd Brutus, I will entertain them.
Fellow, wilt thou bestow thy time with me?

61   bestow : spend.

**Strato**

62   prefer : recommend.

Ay, if Messala will prefer me to you.

**Octavius**
Do so, good Messala.

**Messala**
How died my master, Strato?

**Strato**

67   latest : last.
69   save : except.
71–2   He joined the conspirators only
because he honestly believed that this
was for the general good of all the
people.

65 I held the sword, and he did run on it.

**Messala**
Octavius, then take him to follow thee,
That did the latest service to my master.

**Antony**
This was the noblest Roman of them all;
All the conspirators save only he

73   *the elements*. Elizabethan
physiology taught that the four
elements—earth, air, fire, and water—
were all present in the human body,
and the nature of the man was
determined by which element was
the strongest (excess of fire, for
instance, would give rise to a choleric
temperament or 'humour'). The
perfect nature (which Antony describes
in Brutus) had an equal balance of all
the elements.

70 Did that they did in envy of great Caesar;
He only, in a general honest thought
And common good to all, made one of them.
His life was gentle, and the elements
So mix'd in him, that Nature might stand up

74   *stand up* : i.e. with pride.
76   Let us treat him with the honour
he deserves.

75 And say to all the world, 'This was a man!'

**Octavius**
According to his virtue let us use him,
With all respect and rites of burial.
Within my tent his bones tonight shall lie,

79   *Most . . . soldier* : with full
military honours.
80   field : army.
81   part : share.

Most like a soldier, order'd honourably.

80 So, call the field to rest; and let's away,
To part the glories of this happy day.        [*Exeunt*

# Shakespeare's Plutarch

The following passages are taken from Sir Thomas North's translation (1579) of Plutarch's *Lives of the Greeks and Romans*.[1]

**Act 1, Scene 2**

lines 1–9    At that time the feast *Lupercalia* was celebrated . . . that day there are divers noblemen's sons, young men . . . which run naked through the city, striking in sport them they meet in their way with leather thongs . . . And many noblewomen and gentlewomen also go of purpose to stand in their way, and do put forth their hands to be stricken . . . persuading themselves that, being with child, they shall have good delivery, and also, being barren, that it will make them to conceive with child.      (page 82)

lines 78–133, 233–47    Antonius . . . was one of them that ran this holy course. So, when he came into the market-place, the people made a lane for him to run at liberty; and he came to Caesar and presented him a diadem wreathed about with laurel. Whereupon there rose a cry of rejoicing, not very great, done only by a few appointed for the purpose. But when Caesar refused the diadem, then all the people together made an outcry of joy. Then Antonius offering it him again, there was a second shout of joy, but yet of a few. But when Caesar refused it again the second time, then all the whole people shouted. Caesar having made this proof found that the people did not like of it, and thereupon rose out of his chair, and commanded the crown to be carried unto Jupiter in the Capitol.      (page 83)

lines 191–3    Caesar also had Cassius in great jealousy and suspected him much. Whereupon he said on a time to his friends: 'What will Cassius do, think ye? I like not his pale looks.' Another time when Caesar's friends complained unto him . . . he answered them again 'As for those fat men and smooth-combed heads', quoth he, 'I never reckon of them. But these pale-visaged and carrion lean people, I fear them most.'—meaning Brutus and Cassius.      (page 85)

[1] *Shakespeare's Plutarch*, ed. T. J. B. Spencer (Penguin, 1964). All page references are taken from this edition.

### Act 2, Scene 3 *and* Act 3, Scene 1

lines 6–8   And one Artemidorus . . . [who] was very familiar with certain of
Brutus' confederates and therefore knew the most part of all their
practices against Caesar, came and brought him a little bill written
with his own hand . . . Caesar took it of him, but could never read
it, for the number of people that did salute him.          (page 91)

### Act 3, Scene 1

lines 27–76   So, Caesar coming into the [Senate] house, all the Senate stood up
on their feet to do him honour. Then part of Brutus' company and
confederates stood round about Caesar's chair, and part of them
also came towards him, as though they made suit with Metellus
Cimber, to call home his brother again from banishment; and thus,
prosecuting still their suit, they followed Caesar till he was set in
his chair; who denying their petitions and being offended with
them one after another, because the more they were denied, the
more they pressed upon him and were the earnester with him.
Metellus at length, taking his gown with both his hands, pulled it
over his neck, which was the sign given the confederates to set
upon him.                                              (pages 92–3)
Then Casca behind strake him in the neck with his sword. Howbeit
the wound was not great nor mortal, because, it seemed, the fear
of such a devilish attempt did amaze him and take his strength from
him, that he killed him not at the first blow.          (page 93)
They on the other side that had conspired his death compassed
him in on every side with their swords drawn in their hands, that
Caesar turned him nowhere but he was stricken at by some, and
still had naked swords in his face, and was hacked and mangled
among them, as a wild beast taken of hunters. For it was agreed
among them that every man should give him a wound, because all
their parts should be in this murder.                  (page 94)

line 77   Men report also that Caesar did still defend himself against the
rest, running every way with his body. But when he saw Brutus
with his sword drawn in his hand, then he pulled his gown over
his head and made no more resistance, and was driven, either
casually or purposedly by the counsel of the conspirators, against
the base whereon Pompey's image stood, which ran all of a gore-
blood till he was slain.                              (pages 94–5)

lines 78–121   Brutus and his consorts, having their swords bloody in their hands,
went straight to the Capitol, persuading the Romans, as they went,

to take their liberty again. Now at the first time, when the murder was newly done, there were sudden outcries of people that ran up and down the city; the which indeed did the more increase the fear and tumult . . . Brutus made an oration unto them to win the favour of the people and to justify what they had done. All those that were by said they had done well, and cried unto them that they should boldly come down from the Capitol. Whereupon, Brutus and his companions came boldly down into the market-place. The rest followed in troop; but Brutus went foremost, very honourably compassed in round about with the noblest men of the city, which brought him from the Capitol, through the market-place, to the pulpit for orations. (pages 125–6)

lines 227–35 Then Antonius thinking good his testament should be read openly, and also that his body should be honourably buried and not in hugger-mugger, lest the people might thereby take occasion to be worse offended if they did otherwise, Cassius stoutly spake against it. But Brutus went with the motion, and agreed unto it. Wherein it seemeth he committed a second fault. For the first fault he did was when he would not consent to his fellow conspirators that Antonius should be slain; and therefore he was justly accused that thereby he had saved and strengthened a strong and grievous enemy of their conspiracy. The second fault was when he agreed that Caesar's funerals should be as Antonius would have them; the which indeed marred all. (pages 127–8)

## Act 3, Scene 2

lines 73–258 Afterwards, when Caesar's body was brought into the market-place, Antonius making his funeral oration in praise of the dead, according to the ancient custom of Rome, and perceiving that his words moved the common people to compassion, he framed his eloquence to make their hearts yearn the more; and, taking Caesar's gown all bloody in his hand, he laid it open to the sight of them all, showing what a number of cuts and holes it had upon it. Therewithal the people fell presently into such a rage and mutiny that there was no more order kept amongst the common people. For some of them cried out: 'Kill the murderers'. Others plucked up forms, tables and stalls about the market-place . . . and having laid them all on a heap together, they set them on fire, and thereupon did put the body of Caesar, and burnt it in the middest of the most holy places. And furthermore, when the fire was throughly kindled, some here, some there, took burning fire-brands, and ran with them to the murderers' houses that had killed him, to set them a-fire. Howbeit the conspirators, foreseeing the danger before, had wisely provided for themselves, and fled.          (pages 128–9)

### Act 3, Scene 3

But there was a poet called Cinna, who had been no partaker of the conspiracy but was alway one of Caesar's chiefest friends . . . when he heard that they carried Caesar's body to burial, being ashamed not to accompany his funerals, he went out of his house, and thrust himself into the press of the common people that were in a great uproar. And because some one called him by his name, Cinna, the people thinking he had been that Cinna who in an oration he had made had spoken very evil of Caesar, they falling upon him in their rage slew him outright in the market-place.

(pages 129–30)

### Act 4, Scene 3

lines 1–137  About that time Brutus sent to pray Cassius to come to the city of Sardis; and so he did . . . Now as it commonly happeneth in great affairs between two persons, both of them having many friends and so many captains under them, there ran tales and complaints betwixt them. Therefore . . . they went into a little chamber together, and bade every man avoid, and did shut the doors to them. Then they began to pour out their complaints one to another, and grew hot and loud, earnestly accusing one another, and at length fell both a-weeping . . . [Eventually Marcus Faonius] in despite of the doorkeepers, came into the chamber, and, with a certain scoffing and mocking gesture which he counterfeited of purpose, he rehearsed the verses which old Nestor said in Homer:

> My lords, I pray you hearken both to me,
> For I have seen moe years than suchie three.

Cassius fell a-laughing at him. But Brutus thrust him out of the chamber, and called him dog and counterfeit Cynic. Howbeit his coming in brake their strife at that time; and so they left each other.                                    (pages 145–6)

But, above all, the ghost that appeared unto Brutus showed plainly that the gods were offended with the murder of Caesar. The vision was thus. Brutus . . . slept every night, as his manner was, in his tent; and being yet awake thinking of his affairs—for by report he was as careful a captain and lived with as little sleep as ever man did—he thought he heard a noise at his tent door; and, looking towards the light of the lamp that waxed very dim, he saw a horrible vision of a man, of a wonderful greatness and dreadful look, which at the first made him marvellously afraid. But when he saw that it did him no hurt, but stood by his bedside and said nothing, at length he asked him what he was. The image answered him: 'I am thy ill angel, Brutus, and thou shalt see me by the city of Philippes.' Then Brutus replied again, and said: 'Well, I shall see thee then.' Therewithal the spirit presently vanished from him.

(pages 99–100)

### Act 5, Scene 1

lines 93–125    [Cassius said] 'The gods grant us, O Brutus, that this day we may win the field and ever after to live all the rest of our life quietly one with another. But sith the gods have so ordained it that the greatest and chiefest things amongst men are most uncertain, and that, if the battle fall out otherwise today than we wish or look for, we shall hardly meet again, what art thou then determined to do—to fly, or die?' Brutus answered him:

> 'Being yet a young man and not over greatly experienced in the world, I trust (I know not how) a certain rule of philosophy by the which I did greatly blame and reprove Cato for killing of himself, as being no lawful nor godly act, touching the gods, nor, concerning men, valiant; not to give place and yield to divine providence, and not constantly and patiently to take whatsoever it pleaseth him to send us, but to draw back and fly. But being now in the midst of the danger, I am of a contrary mind. For, if it be not the will of God that this battle fall out fortunate for us, I will look no more for hope, neither seek to make any new supply for war again, but will rid me of this miserable world, and content me with my fortune. For I gave up my life for my country in the Ides of March, for the which I shall live in another more glorious world.'    (pages 154–5)

### Act 5, Scene 5

lines 1–51    Now, the night being far spent, Brutus as he sat bowed towards Clitus one of his men and told him somewhat in his ear, the other answered him not, but fell a-weeping. Thereupon he proved Dardanus, and said somewhat also to him. At length he came to Volumnius himself, and, speaking to him in Greek, prayed him, for the study's sake which brought them acquainted together, that he would help him to put his hand to his sword, to thrust it in him to kill him. Volumnius denied his request, and so did many others. And, amongst the rest, one of them said, there was no tarrying for them there, but that they must needs fly. Then Brutus rising up:

> 'We must fly indeed,' he said, 'but it must be with our hands not with our feet.'

Then, taking every man by the hand, he said these words unto them with a cheerful countenance:

> 'It rejoiceth my heart that not one of my friends hath failed me at my need, and I do not complain of my fortune, but only for my country's sake. For, as for me, I think myself happier than they that have overcome, considering that I leave a perpetual fame of our courage and manhood, the which our enemies the conquerors shall never attain unto by force nor money, neither can let their posterity to say that they, being naughty and unjust men, have slain good men, to usurp tyrannical power not pertaining to them.'

Having said so, he prayed every man to shift for themselves. And then he went a little aside with two or three only, among the which Strato was one ... He came as near to him as he could, and, taking his sword by the hilts with both his hands and falling down upon the point of it, ran himself through. Others say that not he, but Strato, at his request, held the sword in his hand, and turned his head aside, and that Brutus fell down upon it; and so ran himself through, and died presently.                                  (pages 170–2)

lines 68–75    Antonius spake it openly divers times that he thought that of all them that had slain Caesar there was none but Brutus only that was moved to do it as thinking the act commendable of itself; but that all the other conspirators did conspire his death for some private malice or envy that they otherwise did bear unto him.

(page 140)

# Examinations

I know that many of you will have been studying *Julius Caesar* for examination purposes, and I want now to offer some suggestions about the techniques of answering examination questions.

First of all, you must know the play well: that is, you must know what happens in it, what the characters are like, and what the words mean. Then, the most important rule in any kind of examination is: *answer the question*. You will always have far more information to offer than the question asks for; but the purpose of the examination is not simply to test what you know. The examiners want to find out how well you can *use* what you know—how you can select information that is relevant to the question, and how you can organize your material into a coherent and logical argument.

Different examining Boards set different kinds of questions; your teacher will be able to tell you which sort is favoured by your Board. Looking through past papers, I have found three kinds of question—'context' questions, 'comprehension' questions, and essays. I have taken recent specimens of each one of these and tried to show you how I would answer them. Following my 'answers' is a range of questions such as I would set if I were an examiner.

## Specimen Answers

## A   Context questions

These questions present you with short passages from the play, and ask you to explain them. Usually you have to make a choice of passages: there may be five on the paper, and you are asked to choose three. Be very sure that you know exactly how many passages you must choose. Study the ones offered to you, and select those you feel most certain of.

**Question**

> Go, go, good countrymen, and for this fault
> Assemble all the poor men of your sort;
> Draw them to Tiber banks, and weep your tears
> Into the channel, till the lowest stream
> Do kiss the most exalted shores of all.
> See whe'r their basest mettle be not mov'd;

> They vanish tongue-tied in their guiltiness.
> Go you down that way towards the Capitol;
> This way will I. Disrobe the images
> If you do find them deck'd with ceremonies.

(i) Who is speaking? To whom is he speaking in the first part of the speech, and in the second?

(ii) What is the 'fault' he refers to?

(iii) Who else, later in the play, tells these people to weep, and upon what occasion?

(iv) What effect does the speaker hope that the action of disrobing the images will have upon Caesar?

(v) What happens to the speaker as a result of this action?

**Suggested answer**

(i) Flavius is speaking, first to the Roman citizens, and then to his fellow-tribune, Marullus.

(ii) The citizens have shown disloyalty to the memory of Pompey in their welcome to Caesar.

(iii) Mark Antony, at Caesar's funeral.

(iv) Make him more humble and less ambitious.

(v) He is put to death.

**Question**

> Are you not mov'd, when all the sway of earth
> Shakes like a thing unfirm? O Cicero,
> I have seen tempests when the scolding winds
> Have riv'd the knotty oaks, and I have seen
> Th'ambitious ocean swell, and rage, and foam,
> To be exalted with the threat'ning clouds;
> But never till tonight, never till now,
> Did I go through a tempest dropping fire.
> Either there is a civil strife in heaven
> Or else the world, too saucy with the gods,
> Incenses them to send destruction.

(i) Who is speaking to Cicero?

(ii) Give in your own words this character's explanation for the violence of the storm ('Either . . . destruction').

(iii) Who comes on to the stage next? How does he show that he welcomes the storm?

(iv) How does this character explain the storm?

(v) Name one other unusual thing that has been seen during the day of the storm.

**Suggested answer**

(i) Casca.

(ii) Either there is war in heaven and the gods are fighting each other, or else men have not shown respect, which has angered the gods so that they are going to destroy the world.

(iii) Cassius; he wears his doublet unfastened and walks directly in the path of the lightning.

(iv) That the gods intend the unusual events in the natural world (macrocosm) to warn men of something equally unnatural in the world of human affairs (microcosm).

(v) A slave's hand was on fire, yet it did not get burnt.


## B   Comprehension questions

These also present passages from the play and ask questions about them, and again you often have a choice of passages. But the extracts are much longer than those presented as context questions. A detailed knowledge of the language of the play is asked for here, and you must be able to express unusual or archaic phrases in your own words; you may also be asked to comment critically on the effectiveness of Shakespeare's language.

**Question**

*Brutus:*

It must be by his death; and, for my part,
I know no personal cause to spurn at him,
But for the general. He would be crown'd:
How that might change his nature, there's the question:
It is the bright day that brings forth the adder,     5
And that craves wary walking. Crown him? — that!
And then, I grant, we put a sting in him,
That at his will he may do danger with.
The abuse of greatness is when it disjoins
Remorse from power; and, to speak truth of Caesar,   10
I have not known when his affections sway'd
More than his reason. But 'tis a common proof,
That lowliness is young ambition's ladder,
Whereto the climber-upward turns his face;
But when he once attains the upmost round,     15
He then unto the ladder turns his back,
Looks in the clouds, scorning the base degrees
By which he did ascend. So Caesar may:
Then, lest he may, prevent. And, since the quarrel

Will bear no colour for the thing he is,                    20
Fashion it thus: that what he is, augmented,
Would run to these and these extremities;
And therefore think him as a serpent's egg
Which, hatch'd, would, as his kind, grow mischievous,
And kill him in the shell.                    25

    (i) Say concisely where in the play the passage occurs.
    (ii) Give the meaning of *common proof* (line 12) and *prevent* (line 19).
    (iii) Bring out in your own words the meaning of lines 9–10 (*The abuse of greatness . . . power*) and 21–2 (*Fashion . . . extremities*).
    (iv) Show how the ladder metaphor helps to emphasize the point that Brutus is making in this passage.
    (v) Do you find Brutus's reasoning in this passage convincing?

**Suggested answer**
    (i) After Cassius has mentioned his plot to Brutus, and before Cassius brings the conspirators to Brutus's house and Brutus joins them.
    (ii) well-known fact.
       anticipate and stop it from happening.
    (iii) When a great man uses his power without mercy, he is misusing his position of authority.
       Put it this way: if more power is added to what he already has, he will become tyrannous in these particular ways.
    (iv) We often talk about people 'getting to the top of the ladder' when they are successful, and so the ladder metaphor is not unusual. Brutus makes us see a man climbing a real ladder, and it is true that when a person has climbed up to the top he does not look down, because this would in fact be dangerous: he might lose his balance. Because this is true of climbing a *real* ladder, Brutus assumes that it is equally true of climbing a metaphorical ladder, and he deceives himself with his metaphor.
    (v) It is quite clear that Brutus has no evidence to support his claim that Caesar will become a tyrant. Caesar has never injured Brutus, nor been known to act irrationally. Brutus makes some general statements about human nature, and applies these to Caesar without any further justification. He cannot say that Caesar *will* look down on those who helped him, only that he *may*. It is natural for a snake's egg to hatch into a snake, but Brutus has not shown how Caesar is, metaphorically, a snake. Even Brutus is not really convinced by his own arguments, because he says that 'the

quarrel / Will bear no colour for the thing he is', which means that nobody will accept the argument as it really is. So Brutus has to twist his reasoning to make it sound logical. He begins his speech by declaring that Caesar must die, and then tries to find arguments to justify his conclusion; this is quite the wrong way round.

## C Essays

These questions always give you a specific topic to discuss. They *never* want you to tell the story of the whole play—so don't. The examiner has read the play, and does not need to be reminded of it. Give him only what he asks for.

### Question

'O Julius Caesar, thou art mighty yet!
Thy spirit walks abroad, and turns our swords
In our own proper entrails.'
    Give an account of incidents in the play which illustrate this comment.

### Suggested approach to an answer

First, make a list of the material you can draw on for this answer; then make a plan. The plan should be no more than an outline: you do not have time to write a rough draft of your essay and copy it out. Your plan might look like this:

| References to Caesar's spirit after Caesar's death: | Effect of reference: |
|---|---|
| (a) Ant. speaks of C's spirit wanting revenge, immediately after murder | starts off 2nd movement of play |
| (b) A reads C's will | reminds us of generosity & love for citizens—good spirit |
| (c) Brutus reminds Cassius of cause of C's death | we remember different motives of conspirators |
| (d) A reminds Brutus of treachery of murder | we are made more eager to see revenge |
| (e) Cassius sees his own death as part of C's revenge | feel increased power of spirit |
| (f) Brutus seems to welcome death | |

<u>Appearance of Ghost</u>—not surprising after we have heard so much
  about C's spirit

<u>First mention of C's spirit</u>—by Brutus, before Caesar's death,
  when he regrets that they cannot kill spirit without killing body:
  ironically they kill body without killing spirit

<u>Caesar's spirit</u> unifies play, so that it does not fall to pieces after
murder

———————

Can you remember any of the actual words of the play? If you can,
it will help you to make your points more strongly, and show the
examiner that you have indeed studied *the play*, and not just a prose
account of the action and characters. But quotations must always
be relevant. If they are not relevant, it is a waste of time writing
them out; you will get no marks for this.

### Specimen Questions

## A   Context questions

1.     She dreamt tonight she saw my statue,
       Which, like a fountain with a hundred spouts,
       Did run pure blood; and many lusty Romans
       Came smiling, and did bathe their hands in it:
       And these does she apply for warnings and portents,
       And evils imminent.

(i) Who speaks, and to whom does he speak?
(ii) How exactly does the dreamer interpret the dream? What
does she want the speaker to do?
(iii) How does the listener interpret the dream?
(iv) Which is the correct interpretation?

2.     Thou seest the world, Volumnius, how it goes;
       Our enemies have beat us to the pit:
       It is more worthy to leap in ourselves
       Than tarry till they push us.

(i) Who is the speaker?
(ii) What is the occasion?
(iii) What does the speaker ask Volumnius to do, and what
does Volumnius reply?
(iv) What is the speaker's reaction to Volumnius' reply?

3.       The skies are painted with unnumber'd sparks,
They are all fire, and every one doth shine;
But there's but one in all doth hold his place;
So, in the world; 'tis furnish'd well with men,
And men are flesh and blood, and apprehensive,
Yet in the number do I know but one
That unassailable holds on his rank.

(i) Who is speaking, and of whom does he speak?
(ii) What has he been asked to do?
(iii) Does he consent?
(iv) What happens next?

4.                     for this present
I would not, so with love I might entreat you,
Be any further mov'd. What you have said
I will consider; what you have to say
I will with patience hear, and find a time
Both meet to hear and answer such high things.

(i) Who is speaking, and to whom does he speak?
(ii) What is the occasion?
(iii) What are the 'high things' that have been discussed?
(iv) How does the speaker eventually answer them?

5.                  There is my dagger,
And here my naked breast; within, a heart
Dearer than Plutus' mine, richer than gold:
If that thou be'st a Roman, take it forth;
I, that denied thee gold, will give my heart:
Strike, as thou didst at Caesar.

(i) Who is speaking, and where is the scene?
(ii) What has the speaker been accused of?
(iii) By whom has he been accused?
(iv) What is the real cause of the accuser's distress?

6.       Is it excepted I should know no secrets
That appertain to you? Am I yourself
But, as it were, in sort or limitation,
To keep with you at meals, comfort your bed,
And talk to you sometimes?

(i) Who is speaking, and to whom?
(ii) What secret does the speaker want to know?
(iii) What has the speaker just done, and why?
(iv) What happens to the speaker at the end of the play?

## B   Comprehension questions

*Antony:*

7.      I know not, gentlemen, what you intend,
Who else must be let blood, who else is rank:
If I myself, there is no hour so fit
As Caesar's death's hour, nor no instrument
Of half that worth as those your swords, made rich          5
With the most noble blood of all this world.
I do beseech ye, if ye bear me hard,
Now, whilst your purpled hands do reek and smoke,
Fulfil your pleasure. Live a thousand years,
I shall not find myself so apt to die;                       10
No place will please me so, no mean of death,
As here by Caesar, and by you cut off,
The choice and master spirits of this age.

(i) Explain in your own words *bear me hard* (line 7); *apt to die* (line 10); *choice and master spirits* (line 13).

(ii) Comment on the effectiveness of the 'blood-letting' imagery.

(iii) How would you describe Mark Antony's tone in this speech?

(iv) What is the reaction of the characters who hear this speech?

*Cassius:*

8.      He had a fever when he was in Spain,
And when the fit was on him, I did mark
How he did shake; 'tis true, this god did shake;
His coward lips did from their colour fly,
And that same eye whose bend doth awe the world          5
Did lose his lustre; I did hear him groan,
Ay, and that tongue of his, that bade the Romans
Mark him and write his speeches in their books,
Alas, it cried, 'Give me some drink, Titinius',
As a sick girl. Ye gods, it doth amaze me,                 10

A man of such a feeble temper should
So get the start of the majestic world,
And bear the palm alone.

(i) Explain the meaning of *His coward lips did from their colour fly* (line 4); *whose bend doth awe the world* (line 5); *the majestic world* (line 12).

(ii) What impression of Caesar does Cassius hope to give in this speech?

(iii) Do you think he is successful?

(iv) What is happening offstage whilst Cassius is speaking?

*Brutus:*

9.    No, not an oath: if not the face of men,
    The sufferance of our souls, the time's abuse—
    If these be motives weak, break off betimes,
    And every man hence to his idle bed;
    So let high-sighted tyranny rage on,                                    5
    Till each man drop by lottery. But if these,
    As I am sure they do, bear fire enough
    To kindle cowards and to steel with valour
    The melting spirits of women, then, countrymen,
    What need we any spur but our own cause                                 10
    To prick us to redress? what other bond
    Than secret Romans, that have spoke the word
    And will not palter? and what other oath
    Than honesty to honesty engag'd,
    That this shall be, or we will fall for it?                             15

(i) Explain the meaning of *time's abuse* (line 2); *drop by lottery* (line 6); *honesty to honesty engag'd* (line 14).

(ii) How appropriate are the metaphors of fire, steel, and spur to the subject of this speech?

(iii) What impression do we get from these lines of the character of Brutus?

(iv) Which character is set in contrast to Brutus in this scene?

## C  Essay questions

10. Describe the character of Cassius, showing how our attitude to him changes towards the end of the play.
11. On three occasions Brutus refuses to listen to advice from

Cassius; say what these occasions are, and explain Brutus's reasons for not taking the advice.

12. What contributions to the play are made by Calphurnia and Portia?

13. Is Mark Antony a loyal friend to Caesar, or a skilful politician working for his own ends?

14. Give an account of the part played in *Julius Caesar* by the Roman citizens.

15. How important is the supernatural in *Julius Caesar*?

16. How does Shakespeare maintain our interest in the play once its hero, Julius Caesar, is dead?

17. Why do Brutus and Cassius lose the battle at Philippi?

18. Describe some of the different effects achieved by Shakespeare's use of prose in *Julius Caesar*.

# William Shakespeare, 1564–1616

Elizabeth I was Queen of England when Shakespeare was born in 1564. He was the son of a tradesman who made and sold gloves in the small town of Stratford-upon-Avon, and he was educated at the grammar school in that town. Shakespeare did not go to university when he left school, but worked, perhaps, in his father's business. When he was eighteen he married Anne Hathaway, who became the mother of his daughter, Susanna, in 1583, and of twins in 1585.

There is nothing exciting, or even unusual, in this story; and from 1585 until 1592 there are no documents that can tell us anything at all about Shakespeare. But we have learned that in 1592 he was known in London, and that he had become both an actor and a playwright.

We do not know when Shakespeare wrote his first play, and indeed we are not sure of the order in which he wrote his works. If you look on page 113 at the list of his writings and their approximate dates, you will see how he started by writing plays on subjects taken from the history of England. No doubt this was partly because he was always an intensely patriotic man—but he was also a very shrewd business-man. He could see that the theatre audiences enjoyed being shown their own history, and it was certain that he would make a profit from this kind of drama.

The plays in the next group are mainly comedies, with romantic love stories of young people who fall in love with one another, and at the end of the play marry and live happily ever after.

At the end of the sixteenth century the happiness disappears, and Shakespeare's plays become melancholy, bitter, and tragic. This change may have been caused by some sadness in the writer's life (one of his twins died in 1596). Shakespeare, however, was not the only writer whose works at this time were very serious. The whole of England was facing a crisis. Queen Elizabeth I was growing old. She was greatly loved, and the people were sad to think she must soon die; they were also afraid, for the Queen had never married, and so there was no child to succeed her.

When James I came to the throne in 1603, Shakespeare continued to write serious drama—the great tragedies and the plays based on Roman history (such as *Julius Caesar*) for which he is most famous. Finally, before he retired from the theatre, he wrote another set of comedies. These all have the same theme: they tell of happiness which is lost, and then found again.

Shakespeare returned from London to Stratford, his home town. He was rich and successful, and he owned one of the biggest houses in the town. He died in 1616.

Shakespeare also wrote two long poems, and a collection of sonnets. The sonnets describe two love-affairs, but we do not know who the lovers were. Although there are many public documents concerned with his career as a writer and a business-man, Shakespeare has hidden his personal life from us. A nineteenth-century poet, Matthew Arnold, addressed Shakespeare in a poem, and wrote 'We ask and ask—Thou smilest, and art still'.

There is not even a trustworthy portrait of the world's greatest dramatist.

# Approximate order of composition of Shakespeare's works

| Period | Comedies | History plays | Tragedies | Poems |
|---|---|---|---|---|
| I | Comedy of Errors | Henry VI, part 1 | Titus Andronicus | |
| | Taming of the Shrew | Henry VI, part 2 | | |
| | Two Gentlemen of Verona | Henry VI, part 3 | | Venus and Adonis |
| 1594 | | Richard III | | Rape of Lucrece |
| | Love's Labour's Lost | King John | | |
| II | Midsummer Night's Dream | Richard II | Romeo and Juliet | Sonnets |
| | Merchant of Venice | Henry IV, part 1 | | |
| | Merry Wives of Windsor | Henry IV, part 2 | | |
| 1599 | Much Ado About Nothing | | | |
| | As You Like It | Henry V | | |
| III | Twelfth Night | | Julius Caesar | |
| | Troilus and Cressida | | Hamlet | |
| | Measure for Measure | | Othello | |
| 1608 | All's Well That Ends Well | | Timon of Athens | |
| | | | King Lear | |
| | | | Macbeth | |
| | | | Antony and Cleopatra | |
| | | | Coriolanus | |
| IV | Pericles | | | |
| | Cymbeline | | | |
| 1613 | A Winter's Tale | Henry VIII | | |
| | The Tempest | | | |